ALEXANDRIA OCASIO-CORTEZ

ALEXANDRIA OCASIO-CORTEZ

A Biography

Laurie Collier Hillstrom

GREENWOOD BIOGRAPHIES

 GREENWOOD

An Imprint of ABC-CLIO, LLC

Santa Barbara, California • Denver, Colorado

Copyright © 2020 by ABC-CLIO, LLC

All rights reserved. No part of this publication may be reproduced, stored in a retrieval system, or transmitted, in any form or by any means, electronic, mechanical, photocopying, recording, or otherwise, except for the inclusion of brief quotations in a review, without prior permission in writing from the publisher.

Library of Congress Cataloging in Publication Control Number: 2019916680

ISBN: 978-1-4408-7537-3 (print)
       978-1-4408-7538-0 (ebook)

24 23 22 21 20   1 2 3 4 5

This book is also available as an eBook.

Greenwood
An Imprint of ABC-CLIO, LLC

ABC-CLIO, LLC
147 Castilian Drive
Santa Barbara, California 93117
www.abc-clio.com

This book is printed on acid-free paper ∞

Manufactured in the United States of America

CONTENTS

CONTENTS

SERIES FOREWORD

In response to school and library needs, ABC-CLIO publishes this distinguished series of full-length biographies specifically for student use. Prepared by field experts and professionals, these engaging biographies are tailored for students who need challenging yet accessible biographies. Ideal for school assignments and student research, the length, format, and subject areas are designed to meet educators' requirements and students' interests.

ABC-CLIO offers an extensive selection of biographies spanning all curriculum-related subject areas including social studies, the sciences, literature and the arts, history and politics, and popular culture, covering public figures and famous personalities from all time periods and backgrounds, both historic and contemporary, who have made an impact on American and/or world culture. The subjects of these biographies were chosen based on comprehensive feedback from librarians and educators. Consideration was given to both curriculum relevance and inherent interest. Readers will find a wide array of subject choices from fascinating entertainers like Miley Cyrus and Lady Gaga to inspiring leaders like John F. Kennedy and Nelson Mandela, from the greatest athletes of our time like Michael Jordan and Muhammad Ali to the most amazing success stories of our day like J. K. Rowling and Oprah Winfrey.

While the emphasis is on fact, not glorification, the books are meant to be fun to read. Each volume provides in-depth information about the subject's life from birth through childhood, the teen years, and adulthood. A thorough account relates family background and education, traces personal and professional influences, and explores struggles, accomplishments, and contributions. A timeline highlights the most significant life events against a historical perspective. Further Reading sections supplement the reference value of each volume.

INTRODUCTION: A POLITICAL PHENOMENON

The idea that any one person is going to save us is not true. I'm not going to save us. Only we can save us. And I'm only as useful or powerful as the amount of people knocking on doors and talking to their neighbors. (Feller 2018)

Alexandria Ocasio-Cortez—commonly known by her initials, AOC—burst onto the American political scene in June 2018, when the unknown newcomer defeated a powerful ten-term incumbent, Joseph Crowley, in the Democratic primary election to represent New York's Fourteenth Congressional District. Ocasio-Cortez's unexpected triumph over the party establishment catapulted the young, Latina, working-class "girl from the Bronx" and her slate of unapologetically progressive ideas into the national spotlight. Five months later, Ocasio-Cortez cruised to victory in the November midterms to become—at age 29—the youngest woman ever elected to Congress. She joined a "blue wave" that saw historic numbers of women and people of color elected to office and gave the Democratic Party control of the House of Representatives.

Ocasio-Cortez's unlikely ascent captured an inordinate amount of media attention. "There's this 'lightning strikes' quality with Ocasio-Cortez," wrote Katherine Miller of BuzzFeed News, "like for so long, each day, we prayed for something to fight about that isn't [President Donald] Trump, and something that is fun, and when both finally came along in one personage, nobody knew what to do or how to explain her prominence" (Miller 2018). People across the country became captivated by the congresswoman's backstory—her Puerto Rican roots, her family's financial struggles, her achievements as a first-generation college graduate, her experiences as a community organizer, and her employment as a bartender during her campaign—which seemed at once ordinary in the way it reflected the typical life experiences of her constituents, and extraordinary in the way it contrasted with the typical résumé of members of Congress.

As a member of the millennial generation and a native of the digital age, Ocasio-Cortez parlayed the media coverage and public interest into a massive social media presence, collecting 4.5 million followers on Twitter and 3.7 million fans on Instagram within a year of her primary win. Her mastery of social media as a political tool helped her establish a uniquely high profile for a newly elected representative. "We have not seen such a famous freshman member of the House since John Quincy Adams was elected to the House of Representatives after serving as our sixth president of the United States," said MSNBC anchor Lawrence O'Donnell. "And there is apparently no one in the House of Representatives who understands fame and knows how to use fame better than Congresswoman Ocasio-Cortez, who does not need a staff to explain Instagram to her or any other social media or mass communication tool" (Brigham 2019).

Ocasio-Cortez took full advantage of her newfound visibility to amplify her platform of progressive ideas aimed at eliminating economic inequality, achieving social justice, and making the federal government accountable to all citizens rather than only the wealthy and powerful. Ocasio-Cortez's ability to engage social media audiences and dominate the news cycle thrust such policies as Medicare for All, tuition-free public college, the Green New Deal, and abolishing ICE (the U.S. Immigration and Customs Enforcement Agency) to the forefront of public discussion. Some observers credited her influence for pushing the 2020 Democratic presidential candidates—and the entire party platform—to the left.

As Ocasio-Cortez emerged as a leader of the progressive movement, however, the outspoken congresswoman became the target of near-constant attacks from conservative Republicans and right-wing media outlets. Critics portrayed her as either an inexperienced political lightweight or a dangerous radical who threatened to overthrow capitalism and install a socialist system. "Wonder Woman of the left, Wicked Witch of the right, Ocasio-Cortez has become the second most talked-about politician in America, after the President of the United States," Charlotte Alter commented in a *Time* magazine cover story. "She's a political phenomenon: part activist, part legislator, arguably the best storyteller in the party since Barack Obama, and perhaps the only Democrat right now with the star power to challenge President Donald Trump's" (Alter 2019).

Ocasio-Cortez also became a divisive figure among fellow Democrats, as establishment figures and mainstream media outlets debated whether she would prove to be the party's savior or its downfall. Some colleagues resented her celebrity and grumbled that the freshman legislator needed to pay her dues and work within the system. Some moderate Democrats worried that her left-wing agenda might alienate the swing voters the party needed to attract in order to defeat Trump in 2020. Many liberal Democrats, on the other hand, viewed Ocasio-Cortez as the keystone of the party's future appeal to millennials, women, and people of color. "Far beyond policy, she has emerged as a potent symbol for a diversifying Democratic Party: a young woman of color who is giving as good as she gets in a political system that has rarely rewarded people who look like her," Shane Goldmacher wrote in *The New York Times* (Goldmacher 2019).

Some politicians serve for decades without receiving a fraction of the attention Ocasio-Cortez garnered during her first term in office. Following her remarkable rise to political prominence, admirers and detractors alike eagerly awaited the next developments in the congresswoman's career trajectory. "Ocasio-Cortez wants to transform the Democratic Party and the government; she is antiestablishment and ideological in ways that progressives and conservatives understand," Miller stated. "Her successes and failures will mean more, if the last few months have taught us anything, because people want her to prove or disprove something about American politics. Maybe it'll get old, and she'll flame out or fade away—or maybe she won't, and this is the beginning of something unusual" (Miller 2018).

FURTHER READING

Alter, Charlotte. 2019. "'Change Is Closer Than We Think.' Inside Alexandria Ocasio-Cortez's Unlikely Rise." *Time*, March 21, 2019. https://time.com/longform/alexandria-ocasio-cortez-profile/.

Brigham, Bob. 2019. "#WheresMitch: Alexandria Ocasio-Cortez Searches for Missing in Action McConnell as Shutdown Drags On." *Salon*, January 17, 2019. https://www.salon.com/2019/01/17/wheresmitch-alexandria-ocasio-cortez-searches-for-missing-in-action-mcconnell-as-shutdown-drags-on_partner/.

Feller, Madison. 2018. "Alexandria Ocasio-Cortez Knows She Can't Save America All by Herself." *Elle*, July 16, 2018. https://www.elle.com/culture/career-politics/a22118408/alexandria-ocasio-cortez-interview/.

Goldmacher, Shane. 2019. "Ocasio-Cortez Pushes Democrats to the Left, Whether They Like It or Not." *The New York Times*, January 13, 2019. https://www.nytimes.com/2019/01/13/nyregion/ocasio-cortez-democrats-congress.html.

Miller, Katherine. 2018. "Why Alexandria Ocasio-Cortez's Instagram Is So Good." BuzzFeed News, November 21, 2018. https://www.buzzfeednews.com/article/katherinemiller/alexandria-ocasio-cortez-instagram.

TIMELINE

1898   Puerto Rico becomes a U.S. territory at the conclusion of the Spanish American War.

1917   The Jones-Shafroth Act grants American citizenship to residents of Puerto Rico, launching a large-scale migration of Puerto Ricans to the mainland United States.

1987   Representative Nancy Pelosi (D-CA) is elected to her first term in Congress.

1989   October 13—Alexandria Ocasio-Cortez is born in the Bronx borough of New York City.

1994   The Ocasio-Cortez family moves to the Yorktown Heights community in prosperous Westchester County, about forty minutes from the Bronx.

1999   Joseph Crowley is elected to his first term in Congress, representing New York's Fourteenth District.

2001   September 11—Terrorists attack New York City and Washington, D.C., prompting the creation of the Department of Homeland Security and the initiation of wars in Iraq and Afghanistan.

2007 Ocasio-Cortez's high-school microbiology project wins second place globally in the Intel International Science and Engineering Fair. As a reward for her achievement, scientists at the Massachusetts Institute of Technology name an asteroid after Ocasio-Cortez.

Ocasio-Cortez graduates from Yorktown High School.

A global financial crisis sends the U.S. economy spiraling into the Great Recession, which limits employment options and contributes to a student-debt crisis among members of the millennial generation.

2008 Ocasio-Cortez's father, Sergio Ocasio-Roman, dies from a rare form of lung cancer at age 48, putting the family in financial peril.

2011 Ocasio-Cortez graduates from Boston University with a dual degree in international relations and economics.

2016 Ocasio-Cortez serves as a volunteer organizer for Senator Bernie Sanders's progressive campaign seeking the Democratic Party's nomination for president of the United States.

After participating in environmental justice protests in Flint, Michigan, and the Standing Rock Indian Reservation, Ocasio-Cortez experiences a political awakening and decides to run for office.

2017 Ocasio-Cortez launches an insurgent campaign to unseat ten-term incumbent Joseph Crowley in the Democratic primary for New York's Fourteenth Congressional District.

2018 June 18—Crowley receives negative publicity for failing to appear at a scheduled debate with Ocasio-Cortez.

June 26—Ocasio-Cortez sends shockwaves through American politics by roundly defeating Crowley in the primary, 57 percent to 42 percent.

November 6—Ocasio-Cortez cruises to victory in the general election to become the youngest woman ever elected to Congress. She joins a "blue wave" that sees record numbers of women and people of color elected to office and shifts control of the House of Representatives to the Democratic Party.

December 22—Disagreements between President Donald Trump and Congress over border wall funding and other issues precipitate a federal government shutdown.

2019 January 3—Ocasio-Cortez takes the oath of office as a member of the 116th U.S. Congress.

January 15—Ocasio-Cortez joins the House Financial Services Committee.

January 17—At the invitation of the House Democratic Policy and Communications Committee, Ocasio-Cortez gives her Democratic colleagues a tutorial on social media usage.

January 22—Ocasio-Cortez becomes a member of the House Oversight and Reform Committee.

January 25—The longest government shutdown in U.S. history ends when Trump relents on his demand for full border-wall funding.

February 7—Ocasio-Cortez introduces her first piece of legislation, House Resolution 109, "Recognizing the Duty of the Federal Government to Create a Green New Deal."

April 7—A media analysis finds that the conservative news channels Fox News and Fox Business mentioned Ocasio-Cortez 3,181 times—or around 75 times per day—during the previous six weeks.

May—Netflix acquires distribution rights to *Knock Down the House*, a documentary film that provides behind-the-scenes coverage of Ocasio-Cortez's primary campaign, and makes it available for streaming.

June—Ocasio-Cortez amasses 4.5 million followers on Twitter—more than the other sixty newly elected House Democrats combined—as well as 3.7 million fans on Instagram within a year of her primary victory.

July—After visiting immigrant-detention facilities in Texas with a group of Democratic lawmakers, Ocasio-Cortez accuses the U.S. government of operating "concentration camps" on the border.

Chapter 1

BETWEEN TWO WORLDS

I grew up between two worlds, shuttling between the Bronx and Yorktown. . . . It was that experience that allowed me to internalize at an early age that the zip code a child is born in determines much of their opportunity; and that was an early motivating factor for me to work for community change. (Griffith 2018)

Alexandria Ocasio-Cortez's story begins in the Bronx—the northernmost, most populous, and poorest borough of New York City—where her father, Sergio Ocasio-Roman, was born into a working-class family with Puerto Rican roots in 1959. Alexandria's mother, Blanca Ocasio-Cortez, was born in Puerto Rico in 1963. The couple met when Sergio traveled to the island to visit his extended family. After getting married in a Roman Catholic church near the city of Arecibo, they moved to New York to begin a life together. "My parents started from scratch: new languages, new life, new everything," Ocasio-Cortez said (Igoe 2019). The young couple settled in the Bronx neighborhood of Parkchester, a planned community of 171 mid-rise apartment buildings containing 12,000 units that was developed by the Metropolitan Life Insurance Company during World War II.

Sergio owned and operated a small architecture firm, Kirschenbaum Ocasio-Roman PC, that offered remodeling and renovation, building inspection, and landscaping services. Blanca cleaned houses and worked as a secretary. They welcomed their first child, a daughter, on October 13, 1989. "Her dad and I were preparing for Alexandria's birth and still picking names," Blanca recalled, "and he came up with 'Alexandria.' I thought about it for a while and I said: 'Alexandria Ocasio-Cortez. That sounds very powerful. That'll be her name'" (Lambiet 2019). Alexandria's hyphenated surname comes from the convention in Spanish-speaking cultures of giving children the family names of both father (Ocasio) and mother (Cortez). When Alexandria was 2 years old, she gained a younger brother, Gabriel Ocasio-Cortez.

During the early years of Alexandria's childhood, the Ocasio-Cortez family lived in a one-bedroom apartment in the working-class Parkchester community. "We were poor, so I was used to eating rice and beans every day," Ocasio-Cortez remembered. "Also—what do they call it in English? Cream of Wheat. I loved Cream of Wheat. With sugar" (Cadigan 2018). Although they did not have much money, Sergio always insisted on sharing what they had with family, friends, and neighbors. He held an annual pig roast to celebrate his wedding anniversary, for instance, and he always invited extra guests to join the family for holiday meals. "My dad used to say that he collected people," Ocasio-Cortez said. "If you didn't have a place to go on Thanksgiving, you came to our place. We never had a table big enough to fit everyone, but we'd always have folding chairs. You'd make a plate, eat it out of your lap, and share stories" (Cadigan 2018).

From an early age, Alexandria was a bright, talkative, and inquisitive child. At her kindergarten-readiness interview, she dominated the conversation by telling the teachers everything she already knew about letters and numbers. After investigating the underperforming public schools in their Bronx neighborhood, Alexandria's parents decided to seek better educational opportunities for their children. With help from relatives, they purchased a modest, two-bedroom house in Yorktown Heights, a small community in prosperous Westchester County. "My entire extended family—my tias [aunts], my grandparents, everybody—all chipped in so we could get a down payment on a tiny home 40 minutes north of the Bronx, in a school district that was a little bit better than the one I was born into," Ocasio-Cortez said. "It was a reality of my life. That 40-minute drive, from where I went to school to where my family spent their time, kind of told the whole story" (Chávez and Grim 2018).

MOVING BETWEEN THE CITY AND THE SUBURBS

Although she moved a relatively short distance, Ocasio-Cortez went from living in a poor, ethnically diverse urban area with a median annual income of $48,000 to an affluent, mostly white suburb with a median annual income of $116,000 (Griffith 2018). She stayed connected to the Bronx, however, because her father continued working there and her extended family remained in the city. Going back and forth between Westchester County and the Bronx helped her understand the ramifications of income equality. Her experiences in safe, suburban Yorktown Heights stood in stark contrast to those of the cousins she left behind, whom she remembered wearing T-shirts commemorating friends who were killed. "At a very young age I knew it was wrong," she said. "I knew that the fact that my cousins didn't have adequate resources or adequate public services and good schools, and I did, was something that just didn't strike me as right" (Joyce 2018).

With her gregarious nature, Alexandria quickly made friends in her new neighborhood. Their small Yorktown house sat on a half-acre lot, and she enjoyed playing outside. "Alexandria was very social, so she always had a bunch of girls over," her mother remembered. "She took over the shed in the backyard. She cleaned it up, put up curtains and photos and made it look nice, and that was like a clubhouse for her and her friends" (Lambiet 2019). Outside of her friend group, however, some of Alexandria's Yorktown classmates treated her cruelly. "I also grew up as a brown girl in a non-brown environment," she recalled. "I grew up being bullied. I grew up as an ugly duckling in high school. I had jacked-up teeth, and I was really small and gangly, and I had a super awkward phase in middle school, and I had things taken from me" (Feller 2018).

Alexandria often escaped by reading—especially books about history and biographies of individuals who shaped it. Throughout her teen years, she read *The New York Times* every day, disregarding the advice of a teacher who told her that the news was too complex for her to understand. She developed a political perspective by discussing government policy and current events with her family. "Politics were talked about at the table every single day," Alexandria remembered. "It's the culture. In Puerto Rico, you talk about politics all the time, even when people disagree" (Golden 2018). Blanca claimed that her daughter developed her presentation and debate skills during these conversations. "She would engage in political discussions passionately. There was nobody who could shut her up," she recalled. "I saw the political tendencies since she was very, very young" (Newman, Wang, and Ferré-Sadurní 2018).

As a student at Yorktown High School, Alexandria became interested in science, which she viewed as a way to improve people's lives. "She was interested in research to help people in all areas, including developing nations, not just for the people with money," recalled Michael Blueglass, her high-school science teacher (Newman, Wang, and Ferré-Sadurní 2018). Ocasio-Cortez described herself as a "dorky kid" who requested a microscope for a birthday gift and took the commuter train into Spanish Harlem a couple times per week to conduct laboratory experiments at Mount Sinai Medical Center (Alter 2019). In 2007, she entered a project in the Intel International Science and Engineering Fair—the largest science fair in the world for high-school students, with 1,800 entrants selected annually from millions of local competitions in 75 countries. Ocasio-Cortez's project, which examined the effects of antioxidants on the life expectancy of roundworms (nematodes of the species *Caenorhabditis elegans*), took second place globally in the microbiology division.

As a reward for her achievement, scientists with the Lincoln Observatory Near-Earth Asteroid Research (LINEAR) program at the Massachusetts Institute of Technology named an asteroid after Ocasio-Cortez. "Usually science people aren't in the newspaper," said Jenifer Evans, one of the lead engineers at LINEAR. "This is a way to encourage an interest in science because local newspapers will write up, 'Tommy Smith had an asteroid after him.' It's almost as cool as, 'Tommy Smith made three touchdowns at the football game'" (Mosher 2018). Asteroid 23238 Ocasio-Cortez is approximately 1.5 miles wide and follows a stable, oval-shaped orbit around the sun every four years. It travels in the zone between Mars and Jupiter, an average of 240 million miles from Earth.

The local board of education recognized Ocasio-Cortez by inviting her to present her project at a public meeting, where her polished performance impressed everyone in attendance. "One of the administrators wasn't there at the beginning and came in after she started, and he said to the superintendent, 'What company is she from?'" Blueglass remembered. "The superintendent said, 'She's a 17-year-old senior in our high school.' She presented herself, verbally, visually, everything, as if she was a 30-year-old professional presenter businesswoman even though she was 17 years old" (Newman, Wang, and Ferré-Sadurní 2018).

GAINING PERSPECTIVE

Although Ocasio-Cortez took full advantage of the opportunities she gained by moving to Yorktown Heights, it strained the family's finances. Her mother worked long hours at multiple jobs to help pay the bills. "Mami mopped floors, drove school buses, and answered phones," Alexandria remembered. "She did whatever she needed to do, for me" (Igoe 2019). When Blanca cleaned neighbors' homes, Alexandria often joined her to help scrub toilets and wash windows. The teenager also worked as a hostess at an Irish pub to earn money to pay for her extracurricular activities. When conservative critics later accused Ocasio-Cortez of exaggerating her family's struggles for political gain, she noted that her upbringing differed from the typical experience of her peers in Westchester County. "The thing that people don't realize is that wherever there is affluence, there's an underclass," she said. "There's a service class. And that's what I grew up in" (Cadigan 2018).

Like other members of the millennial generation, Ocasio-Cortez came of age during challenging times for the United States. She was 11 years old when the terrorist attacks of September 11, 2001, struck New York City and Washington, D.C., prompting the creation of the Department of Homeland Security and the initiation of wars in Iraq and Afghanistan. She turned 18 as a global financial crisis sent the U.S. economy spiraling into the Great Recession, which limited employment options and contributed to a student-debt crisis. These events colored millennials' perceptions of America as a land of opportunity where people who were willing to work hard could get ahead. Instead, they saw inequity and hardship. "Our whole adolescence was shaped by war, was shaped by the increased erosion of our civil liberties and privacy rights, and then was shaped as soon as we got into college by a ground-shaking recession that has haunted our economic outcomes ever since," Ocasio-Cortez noted (Relman 2019). "An entire generation, which is now becoming one of the largest electorates in America, came of age and never saw American prosperity. I have never seen that, or experienced it, really, in my adult life" (Alter 2019).

Nevertheless, Ocasio-Cortez always maintained the view that the people had the power to change the direction of the country. She credited her father for instilling her with a sense of optimism about American democracy when she accompanied him and his friends on a visit to Washington, D.C., as a child. "Three burly men and a five-year-old in a sedan," she recalled. "One day, his buddies went to get a beer or something, and he took me to the reflecting pool of the Washington Monument. I put my toes in the water, and suddenly the goldfish started to nibble my toes. It was a beautiful day, the sun was out, totally clear. And my dad pointed to all of it—the reflecting pool, the monuments, the Capitol, and he said, 'You know, this is *our* government. All of this belongs to us. It belongs to you'" (Remnick 2018).

PUERTO RICANS IN NEW YORK CITY

When Ocasio-Cortez's parents settled in New York City, they joined a large and thriving community of people of Puerto Rican descent. Puerto Rico became a U.S. territory in 1898, at the conclusion of the Spanish-American War. The large-scale migration of Puerto Rican residents to the mainland United States began with the passage of the Jones-Shafroth Act of 1917, which granted American citizenship to island residents. Migration occurred in several waves after World War II, resulting in the growth of the

Puerto Rican population of New York City from 61,000 in 1940 to 818,000 in 1970.

Although most Puerto Rican migrants came to New York seeking job opportunities, others came in response to hardships caused by hurricanes, crop failures, and financial crises on the island. Facing language barriers and discrimination from city residents of longer standing, they formed tight-knit communities or barrios in certain neighborhoods. Puerto Ricans constituted a majority of the population of the South Bronx, the Lower East Side (Loisaida), East Harlem (known as Spanish Harlem), and the Williamsburg neighborhood in Brooklyn. By 1990, when they comprised 12 percent of the city's total population, people of Puerto Rican descent became known as Nuyoricans.

Within Puerto Rican communities, there are often differences between island-born and mainland-born residents in terms of identity, language, customs, and degree of assimilation. Yet many residents proudly claim their Puerto Rican heritage—some like to refer to themselves as Boricua, a term of profound ethnic pride—and evidence of the island's cultural influence abounds in New York City's music, art, literature, and cuisine. The Puerto Rican Day Parade, held annually since 1958, is one of the largest cultural events in the United States, with two million joining the celebration along Fifth Avenue. "To be Puerto Rican is to be the descendant of: African Moors and slaves, Taino Indians, Spanish colonizers, Jewish refugees, and likely others," Ocasio-Cortez wrote on Twitter. "We are all of these things and something else all at once—we are Boricua" (Cummings 2018).

FURTHER READING

Alter, Charlotte. 2019. "'Change Is Closer Than We Think': Inside Alexandria Ocasio-Cortez's Unlikely Rise." *Time*, March 21, 2019. http://time.com/longform/alexandria-ocasio-cortez-profile/.

Cadigan, Hilary. 2018. "Alexandria Ocasio-Cortez Learned Her Most Important Lessons from Restaurants." *Bon Appetit*, November 7,

2018. https://www.yahoo.com/lifestyle/alexandria-ocasio-cortez-learned-her-141500873.html.

Chávez, Aida, and Ryan Grim. 2018. "A Primary against the Machine: A Bronx Activist Looks to Dethrone Joseph Crowley, the King of Queens." *The Intercept*, May 22, 2018. https://theintercept.com/2018/05/22/joseph-crowley-alexandra-ocasio-cortez-new-york-primary/.

Cummings, William. 2018. "Incoming Congresswoman Ocasio-Cortez Reveals Jewish Ancestry at New York Hanukkah Event." *USA Today*, December 11, 2018. https://www.usatoday.com/story/news/politics/onpolitics/2018/12/11/ocasio-cortez-reveals-jewish-ancestry/2275410002/.

Feller, Madison. 2018. "Alexandria Ocasio-Cortez Knows She Can't Save America All by Herself." *Elle*, July 16, 2018. https://www.elle.com/culture/career-politics/a22118408/alexandria-ocasio-cortez-interview/.

Golden, Hannah. 2018. "28-Year-Old Alexandria Ocasio-Cortez Is Pushing for Millennials' Future through Politics." *Elite Daily*, June 12, 2018. https://www.elitedaily.com/p/28-year-old-alexandria-ocasio-cortez-is-pushing-for-millennials-future-through-politics-9346653.

Griffith, Keith. 2018. "I Grew Up between Two Worlds." *Daily Mail*, July 2, 2018. https://www.dailymail.co.uk/news/article-5908173/Bronx-candidate-Alexandria-Ocasio-Cortez-blasts-questions-working-class-roots.html.

Igoe, Katherine J. 2019. "Who Is Blanca Ocasio-Cortez, Alexandria Ocasio-Cortez's Mom?" *Marie Clarie*, January 30, 2019. https://www.marieclaire.com/politics/a26099099/who-is-alexandria-ocasio-cortez-mom-blanca/.

Joyce, A. P. 2018. "Meet the Young Progressive Latina Trying to Oust One of the Most Powerful Democrats in the House." *Mic*, February 28, 2018. https://mic.com/articles/187994/meet-the-young-progressive-latina-trying-to-oust-one-of-the-most-powerful-democrats-in-the-house#.08z6OhhQS.

Lambiet, Jose. 2019. "Exclusive: 'God Played Quite a Joke on Me with This Politics Stuff.'" *Daily Mail*, March 4, 2019. https://www.dailymail.co.uk/news/article-6748793/Alexandria-Ocasio-

Cortezs-mother-tells-hopes-daughter-marries-longtime-boyf
riend.html.

Mosher, Dave. 2018. "Alexandria Ocasio-Cortez, the 28-Year-Old Who
Defeated a Powerful House Democrat, Has an Asteroid Named after
Her—Here's Why." *Business Insider*, June 28, 2018. https://www
.businessinsider.com/alexandria-ocasio-cortez-asteroid-2018-6.

Newman, Andy, Vivian Wang, and Luis Ferré-Sadurní. 2018. "Alexandria Ocasio-Cortez Emerges as a Political Star." *The New York
Times*, June 27, 2018. https://www.nytimes.com/2018/06/27/nyre
gion/alexandria-ocasio-cortez-bio-profile.html.

Relman, Eliza. 2019. "The Truth about Alexandria Ocasio-Cortez."
Insider, January 6, 2019. https://www.thisisinsider.com/alexand
ria-ocasio-cortez-biography-2019-1.

Remnick, David. 2018. "Alexandria Ocasio-Cortez's Historic Win and
the Future of the Democratic Party." *The New Yorker*, July 16, 2018.
https://www.newyorker.com/magazine/2018/07/23/alexandria-
ocasio-cortezs-historic-win-and-the-future-of-the-democratic-
party.

Chapter 2

FIRST-GENERATION COLLEGE GRADUATE

Greatness has never been a result of circumstance or fortune. It is not an inherited trait or a function of destiny. Greatness is reserved for the delinquents, the combatants of the status quo. (Relman 2019)

After graduating from Yorktown High School in 2007, Alexandria Ocasio-Cortez matriculated to Boston University (BU). Founded in 1839, BU is a private, nonsectarian school with a total enrollment of around 33,000 students. Its 135-acre campus is located on the bank of the Charles River near downtown Boston, Massachusetts, around 200 miles northeast of New York City. Ocasio-Cortez used a combination of scholarships, student loans, and work-study income to finance her college education. She earned a small scholarship from Intel through her strong performance in the Intel International Science and Engineering Fair. She also received a John F. Lopez Fellowship from the National Hispanic Institute (NHI) in recognition of her leadership potential and commitment to serving the Latino community.

Ocasio-Cortez first became involved with the NHI during high school. This nonprofit organization provides learning experiences to students as a means of developing their skills and talents to create future leaders for the Latino community in the United States. While at Yorktown High School, Ocasio-Cortez participated in the Lorenzo de Zavala (LDZ) Youth Legislative Session, a week-long, interactive leadership game in which 10th and 11th-grade students "learn how to navigate, manage and create large organizations by taking charge of your own youth government and proposing future community policies and projects" (National Hispanic Institute 2019). As an undergraduate at BU, she served as secretary of state for the LDZ.

COPING WITH A FAMILY CRISIS

In the fall of 2008, as Ocasio-Cortez entered her sophomore year at BU, her father died from a rare form of lung cancer. Sergio's death at the age of 48 came as a shock, especially because he had never smoked cigarettes and did not have any other known risk factors. Since he died without a will, matters involving his estate had to be settled by a probate court. The probate process ended up being long, complicated, expensive, and stressful for the Ocasio-Cortez family. Through a combination of legal fees, medical bills, and the recession affecting the U.S. economy, they came close to losing their house in Westchester County. Without Sergio's income, Blanca had to work multiple jobs to prevent the banks from foreclosing on the property. "It was scary," Blanca remembered. "I had to stop paying for the mortgage for almost a year. I was expecting someone knocking on the door to kick me out at any time. There were even real estate people coming around to take photos of the house for when it was going to be auctioned" (Lambiet 2019).

Meanwhile, according to Ocasio-Cortez, court-appointed attorneys with political connections enriched themselves at her family's expense. "We entered something known as the surrogates court, otherwise casually known as the 'widows and orphans court,'" she recalled. "Being appointed as a lawyer to the surrogates court, you then rake in the legal fees for all of these families that come through. . . . My father pretty much died with nothing. He left us almost nothing except we had a house and small things here and there. So when you sell that home and all that stuff happens, every time you go through that court, you get these legal fees kind of shaved off. . . . Unfortunately, many people find themselves in this situation" (Scahill 2018).

Ocasio-Cortez described the impact of losing her father as "destabilizing in every way." Each member of the family struggled to cope with the grief on their own terms. "My mother was *done*. My brother was *lost*," she recalled. "I took it hard, too, but I channeled it into my studies. That's how I dealt with it. I was home for a week and went right back to school" (Remnick 2018). Ocasio-Cortez's final visit with her father in the hospital inspired her to work hard to honor his legacy. "I didn't know that it was going to be the last time that I talked to my dad, but toward the end of our interaction, I started to feel like it was," she remembered. "I said goodbye, but I think he knew, and I knew. And so I started to leave, and he kind of hollered out, and I turned around in the doorframe, and he said, 'Hey, make me proud'" (Alter 2019). Ocasio-Cortez returned to BU with a new level of academic commitment, and "she jumped from having good grades to being on the dean's list," her mother stated (Newman, Wang, and Ferré-Sadurní 2018).

SHIFTING FOCUS

Ocasio-Cortez started out majoring in biochemistry at BU with an eventual plan of going to medical school and becoming a doctor. With that goal in mind, she spent a semester abroad in Niger, a developing nation in West Africa. Niger consistently ranks near the bottom of the United Nations Human Development Index, a statistical comparison of nearly 190 countries based on per capita income, education, and life expectancy. With most of its land area covered by the Sahara Desert, Niger struggles with drought, famine, poverty, and poor education and health care systems. Ocasio-Cortez spent four months working in a maternity clinic outside the capital city of Niamey, helping midwives deliver babies in primitive and often unsanitary conditions. "I saw a lot of pretty brutal things there," she acknowledged. One of the experiences that affected her most strongly involved a stillborn infant. "The reason the child had passed was very preventable," she noted. "For me it was a very powerful moment. This child's life was literally decided because of where it was born" (Cadigan 2018).

Although she knew she could help people by practicing medicine, Ocasio-Cortez realized that she could potentially help even more people by approaching health care issues from a broader, societal perspective. Contracting malaria in West Africa reinforced her shift in focus. "In the developing world, malaria is an economic disease," she explained. "It's a disease that impacts so many people as to be actually impacting national GDP, so I started thinking about these health issues as more macro-economic public-policy issues" (Morris 2019). After returning to BU, Ocasio-Cortez changed her major to economics and international relations.

Ocasio-Cortez got a firsthand look at the impact of government policy on individuals' lives while working part-time in the Boston office of U.S. Senator Edward ("Ted") Kennedy (1932–2009). A younger brother of President John F. Kennedy, the long-serving liberal Democrat became known as "The Lion of the Senate" for his contribution to the passage of more than 300 laws. Although Ocasio-Cortez was hired to help Kennedy's staff process requests and respond to complaints from constituents, she wound up dealing primarily with immigration issues. "I was the only Spanish speaker, and as a result, as basically a kid—a 19-, 20-year-old kid—whenever a frantic call would come into the office because someone is looking for their husband because they have been snatched off the street by ICE [U.S. Immigration and Customs Enforcement], I was the one that had to pick up that phone," Ocasio-Cortez recalled. "I was the one that had to help that person navigate that system" (Joyce 2018). Fielding these phone calls helped Ocasio-Cortez understand the challenges facing undocumented people under federal immigration policies.

CAMPUS INVOLVEMENT AND COMMUNITY SERVICE

With her growing interest in public policy and community service, Ocasio-Cortez became involved in several campus organizations that support the interests of minority communities. She served as president of the BU chapter of Alianza Latina, a student-run organization that sponsors social, cultural, political, and community-service events. She also acted as a student ambassador at BU's Howard Thurman Center for Common Ground, which promotes an inclusive learning environment for students from different backgrounds.

Through her work at the Thurman Center, Ocasio-Cortez frequently participated in a wide-ranging weekly discussion forum called

Coffee and Conversations. BU students and faculty members would get together for two hours on Friday afternoons to debate current events and philosophical questions, covering topics ranging from economic inequality and the Affordable Care Act to the meaning of love and the existence of God. Ocasio-Cortez—who went by the nickname "Sandy" during her college years—impressed many other participants with her insightful comments and in-depth knowledge of the issues. "Sandy is brilliant—she is boldly curious and always present," said Kenneth Elmore, the BU dean of students who often hosted the discussions. "She makes me think and could always see multiple sides of any issue" (Barlow 2018).

Raul Fernandez, who served as assistant director of the Thurman Center at BU, remembered Ocasio-Cortez as possessing a "rare combination of heart, smarts, and the ability to use her voice to bring people together" (Barlow 2018). "She was always up for a good debate," he added, "but not before hearing someone else" (Capelouto 2018). Her BU classmate Bruna Maia recalled Ocasio-Cortez's contributions to the sessions as being "a little bit edgy," noting that "she wasn't afraid to take us to the next level" (Relman 2019). As another outcome of the Coffee and Conversations sessions, Ocasio-Cortez met her long-term boyfriend, Arizona native Riley Roberts. After graduating from BU with degrees in sociology and finance, he launched a career as a website developer and real-estate marketing consultant.

Before she graduated from college, Ocasio-Cortez also became involved in grassroots community organizing with students from other nearby institutions, such as Harvard University, the Massachusetts Institute of Technology, Boston College, and Northeastern University. She organized meetings to discuss issues relevant to people poised to enter the workforce, including the financial crisis, income inequality, and student debt. Many participants in the sessions found Ocasio-Cortez inspiring and predicted that she would run for elected office someday. "We would say 'Sandy for president' because we were, like, 'Yes, you're speaking my truth right now,'" Maia remembered (Relman 2019). Mina Vahedi, a BU graduate who lived on the same floor as Ocasio-Cortez in the Warren Towers residence hall freshman year, noted that "she just has this energy that's so motivated and ready just to work and make things happen" (Relman 2019).

Ocasio-Cortez expressed surprise that her peers felt that she had something valuable to contribute. "I didn't understand why people called me an activist," she stated. "I felt like I was just saying things that were very common sense. I would just say, 'Hey, kids in the Bronx should have a good education.' And they'd be, like, 'Oh, she's an activist.' And I was, like, why is it when I say these things I'm an activist, but when this person says these things they're just a responsible parent or auntie or whatever?" (Relman 2019). In January 2011, during her senior year, Ocasio-Cortez was invited to speak at BU's annual Martin Luther King Day observance. She used the occasion to challenge fellow students to live up to King's legacy. "How can we be great?" she asked. "The first step is a choice. King made a conscious decision. Ask yourself, today, how will you be great? In this moment, how am I great?" (Capelouto 2018).

Ocasio-Cortez graduated from BU's College of Arts and Sciences in 2011 with a dual degree in international relations and economics. She ranked fourth in her graduating class, earning cum laude honors, and became the first person in her family to earn a degree. By the time she completed her studies, she had accumulated around $25,000 in student loan debt, which meant she would be saddled with payments of $300 per month for the next decade. Ocasio-Cortez understood, through personal experience, the impact that student debt had on the economic prospects of 44 million other millennials at the outset of their careers. "We have an entire generation that is delaying or forgoing purchasing houses," she stated. "Our entire economy is slowing down due to the student-loan crisis" (Alter 2019). Finding ways to make college education more affordable eventually ranked among her top political priorities.

RILEY ROBERTS

Ocasio-Cortez met her longtime boyfriend, Riley Roberts, while they were both undergraduate students at Boston University. She claimed they got together "in true nerdy fashion" while attending the weekly Coffee and Conversations sessions on campus (Aleksander 2018). Roberts grew up in Paradise Valley, Arizona. He attended Chaparral High School in Scottsdale, where he excelled in debate before graduating in 2008. Roberts went on to earn degrees in sociology and finance from Boston University. After completing his education in 2012, Roberts worked in marketing for HomeBinder, an online home-management service based in New York City. When he and Ocasio-Cortez temporarily broke up, he returned home to Arizona, where he developed websites for small business clients.

Roberts moved back to New York City in 2015, when he and Ocasio-Cortez resumed their relationship. They lived together in a one-bedroom apartment in the Parkchester neighborhood of the Bronx, where she had spent her early childhood. Although Ocasio-Cortez works to keep information about her personal life private, Roberts played an active role in her congressional campaign, and the bearded redhead stood behind her as she took her oath of office. Her mother made headlines by telling an interviewer that she hoped her daughter would marry Roberts. "I love him," Blanca said. "He is the most loving, supporting person I've seen. He helped her tremendously during the election. . . . I know they love children, and they do very well with children from the family. So, I hope they get married soon. Although they haven't told me anything about their plans" (Lambiet 2019).

FURTHER READING

Aleksander, Irina. 2018. "How Alexandria Ocasio-Cortez and Other Progressives Are Defining the Midterms." *Vogue*, October 15, 2018. https://www.vogue.com/article/alexandria-ocasio-cortez-interview-vogue-november-2018-issue.

Alter, Charlotte. 2019. "'Change Is Closer than We Think': Inside Alexandria Ocasio-Cortez's Unlikely Rise." *Time*, March 21, 2019. http://time.com/longform/alexandria-ocasio-cortez-profile/.

Barlow, Rich. 2018. "BU Alumna Wins Upset Congressional Primary in New York City." *BU Today*, June 27, 2018. http://www.bu.edu/today/2018/alexandria-ocasio-cortez-wins-congressional-primary-in-new-york-city/.

Cadigan, Hilary. 2018. "Alexandria Ocasio-Cortez Learned Her Most Important Lessons from Restaurants." *Bon Appetit*, November 7, 2018. https://www.yahoo.com/lifestyle/alexandria-ocasio-cortez-learned-her-141500873.html.

Capelouto, J. D. 2018. "Alexandria Ocasio-Cortez's Friends in Boston Recall Her Drive and Dedication." *Boston Globe*, June 27, 2018. https://www.bostonglobe.com/metro/2018/06/27/alexandria-ocasio-cortez-friends-boston-recall-her-drive-and-dedication-helping-people/rhUi19hDhN2TKcxUP6fGlJ/story.html.

Joyce, A. P. 2018. "Meet the Young Progressive Latina Trying to Oust One of the Most Powerful Democrats in the House." *Mic*, February 28, 2018. https://mic.com/articles/187994/meet-the-young-progressive-latina-trying-to-oust-one-of-the-most-powerful-democrats-in-the-house#.08z6OhhQS.

Lambiet, Jose. 2019. "Exclusive: 'God Played Quite a Joke on Me with This Politics Stuff.'" *Daily Mail*, March 4, 2019. https://www.dailymail.co.uk/news/article-6748793/Alexandria-Ocasio-Cortezs-mother-tells-hopes-daughter-marries-longtime-boyfriend.html.

Morris, Alex. 2019. "Alexandria Ocasio-Cortez Wants the Country to Think Big." *Rolling Stone*, February 27, 2019. https://www.rollingstone.com/politics/politics-features/alexandria-ocasio-cortez-congress-interview-797214/.

National Hispanic Institute. 2019. "Lorenzo de Zavala Youth Legislative Session." National Hispanic Institute. https://www.nationalhispanicinstitute.org/ldz/.

Newman, Andy, Vivian Wang, and Luis Ferré-Sadurní. 2018. "Alexandria Ocasio-Cortez Emerges as a Political Star." *The New York Times*, June 27, 2018. https://www.nytimes.com/2018/06/27/nyregion/alexandria-ocasio-cortez-bio-profile.html.

Relman, Eliza. 2019. "The Truth about Alexandria Ocasio-Cortez." *Insider*, January 6, 2019. https://www.thisisinsider.com/alexandria-ocasio-cortez-biography-2019-1.

Remnick, David. 2018. "Alexandria Ocasio-Cortez's Historic Win and the Future of the Democratic Party." *The New Yorker*, July 16, 2018. https://www.newyorker.com/magazine/2018/07/23/alexandria-ocasio-cortezs-historic-win-and-the-future-of-the-democratic-party.

Scahill, Jeremy. 2018. "An Interview with Alexandria Ocasio-Cortez, the Young Democratic Socialist Who Just Shocked the Establishment." *The Intercept*, June 27, 2018. https://theintercept.com/2018/06/27/an-interview-with-alexandria-ocasio-cortez-the-young-democratic-socialist-who-just-shocked-the-establishment/.

Chapter 3

COMMUNITY ORGANIZER AND RESTAURANT WORKER

The food industry is the nexus . . . of minimum wage fights, of immigration law, of criminal justice reform, of health care debates, of education. You'd be hard-pressed to find a political issue that doesn't have food implications. (Cadigan 2018)

After earning degrees in economics and international relations in 2011, Alexandria Ocasio-Cortez had a variety of employment options available to her. An obvious choice would have been seeking a high-powered job with a transnational corporation or a Wall Street investment firm, but these career paths held no appeal for the recent graduate. "I just physically couldn't do it," she admitted. "I knew it would kill me on the inside" (Relman 2019). Ocasio-Cortez felt a calling to give back to her community and promote social change. She also wanted to support her mother, who had been struggling to prevent foreclosure on their home while ensuring that her two children had the opportunity to go to college. Ocasio-Cortez thus decided to return to the Parkchester neighborhood where she was born. "As soon as I graduated college and had a choice of my own, I moved back home to the Bronx to work in the community and be with my family to help raise the little ones in my family," she recalled (Griffith 2018).

Over the next few years, Ocasio-Cortez became involved in a number of different entrepreneurial and community-service ventures. She worked as an educational strategist for GAGEis, Inc., a consulting firm that offered strategic planning, web design, and copywriting services to help clients in the education sector connect students with careers. She also partnered with the Sunshine Bronx Business Incubator to develop training materials for entrepreneurs hoping to launch new business enterprises in the borough. Ocasio-Cortez started her own small business, a publishing company called Brook Avenue Press. She focused on publishing children's books by urban authors and artists that portrayed life in the Bronx in a positive manner.

Ocasio-Cortez also continued her work with the National Hispanic Institute (NHI) after college. "She's never stopped caring about our work and mission," said NHI senior vice president Julio Cotto. "Somehow, she finds the time to share her wealth of talents with others. She's helped us train, run programs, and be part of the thinking behind NHI's success" (National Hispanic Institute 2017). In 2017, Ocasio-Cortez served as an educational director for the Northeast Collegiate World Series, a five-day program that prepares high-school students to succeed in college. The students receive hands-on learning experiences to help them live independently, manage time effectively, spend money wisely, and make smart decisions relating to their future.

WORKING IN THE FOOD-SERVICE INDUSTRY

Ocasio-Cortez supplemented her income by working as a bartender and server at Flats Fix Taco y Tequila Bar, a hip restaurant in a former garage space near Union Square in Manhattan. Since she knew many other recent college graduates who pieced together multiple part-time jobs or did freelance work to make ends meet, she did not view her situation as unusual. In addition to food, rent, utilities, and other basic living expenses, Ocasio-Cortez paid over $500 per month for student loans and a high-deductible health insurance plan through the Affordable Care Act's marketplace. She thus joined the 78 percent of Americans who work full time yet live from paycheck to paycheck, unable to accumulate enough savings to cover emergency expenses (Remnick 2018). "Try living with the anxiety of not having health insurance for three years when your tooth starts to hurt," she noted. "It's this existential dread. I have that perspective. I feel like I understand what's happening electorally because I have experienced it myself" (Cadigan 2018).

Ocasio-Cortez found working in the food-service industry to be a valuable learning experience. Waiting tables and mixing drinks gave her a better understanding of human nature as well as practice communicating with a wide range of people. "I got really, really, really good at listening to people," she recalled, "and I got really good at understanding people's needs, beyond just food and drink" (Cadigan 2018). At the same time, dealing with difficult customers and experiencing sexual harassment on the job helped Ocasio-Cortez learn to stand up for herself and defuse tense situations. "You get used to people putting themselves above you all the time," she said. "You really start to realize that a person who's treating you badly is really just expressing a problem with themselves" (Relman 2019).

In many ways, Ocasio-Cortez found that restaurant work helped prepare her to become a community organizer and to eventually launch a career in politics. "The thing that people don't understand about restaurants is that they're one of the most political environments," she explained. "You're shoulder-to-shoulder with immigrants. You're at one of the nexuses of income inequality. Your hourly wage is even less than the minimum wage. You're working for tips. You're getting sexually harassed. You see how our food is processed and handled. You see how the prices of things change. It was a very galvanizing political experience for me" (Morris 2019).

For instance, Ocasio-Cortez gained a deeper, more personal understanding of the political issues surrounding immigration by working in the food-service industry. Many restaurants experience problems recruiting dishwashers, bussers, cashiers, and other employees willing to work long hours for low wages. Some restaurants—along with some commercial farms and food-processing facilities—address labor shortages by hiring undocumented immigrants to fill low-paying jobs. Studies suggest that undocumented people perform one-third of all food-service jobs in the United States (Cadigan 2018). Ocasio-Cortez worked alongside both documented and undocumented immigrants at various times, heard their stories, and learned how the threat of raids and arrests by ICE (U.S. Immigration and Customs Enforcement) created fear and uncertainty in their lives.

CAMPAIGNING FOR BERNIE SANDERS

As she gained greater awareness of the challenges facing working-class people and immigrants, Ocasio-Cortez grew more committed to progressive political priorities, such as labor rights, workplace protections, universal health care, and economic equality. In 2016, she became a volunteer organizer for Senator Bernie Sanders (I-VT), who launched a progressive campaign seeking the Democratic Party's nomination for president of the United States. "I had done grassroots organizing before," Ocasio-Cortez noted. "But Sanders' race was one of my first times where I crossed that bridge from grassroots community organizing to electoral organizing" (Alter 2019).

When Sanders launched his campaign for the Democratic presidential nomination, his platform featured many progressive ideas that held strong appeal for Ocasio-Cortez. Sanders proposed increasing the federal minimum wage to $15 per hour, expanding the federal Medicare program to provide health care coverage to all Americans, granting young people access to a free public college education, and taking decisive action to address global climate change. He also advocated policies intended to reduce income inequality and decrease the influence of money in politics. "The major issue is: How do we create an economy that works for all of our people, rather than a small number of billionaires?" Sanders said (Kane and Rucker 2015). To emphasize this point, Sanders rejected large donations from wealthy donors, corporations, and political action committees and relied on small donations from individual voters to finance his campaign.

As an organizer for the Sanders campaign, Ocasio-Cortez established a Bronx headquarters in a former nail salon and used it as a base to promote his candidacy to voters in her community. She made phone calls, knocked on doors, organized rallies, and employed social media tools to spread Sanders's message and help get out the vote. She also worked to generate support for Sanders among progressive groups in New York City, including labor unions, feminists, environmentalists, Black Lives Matter activists, and LGBTQ leaders.

Although most political observers viewed Sanders as a longshot to win the nomination over favorite Hillary Clinton—the former secretary of state, U.S. senator, and First Lady—his campaign attracted enthusiastic support among liberal Democrats who sought a more progressive alternative. With the help of volunteer organizers like Ocasio-Cortez, Sanders ended up winning 23 primaries and receiving 13.2 million popular votes, although his 1,865 delegates fell short of the total needed to claim the nomination. In July 2016, Sanders endorsed Clinton as the Democratic nominee and encouraged his supporters to vote for her in a show of party unity. Some political analysts noted that the eventual Democratic Party platform reflected many of Sanders's popular campaign pledges, including raising the minimum wage and offering free college tuition.

ALIGNING WITH DEMOCRATIC SOCIALISTS

Although Sanders's presidential bid ended in the Democratic primaries, many of his supporters remained energized and determined to build upon the momentum generated by his campaign. In April 2016, some campaign staff members and volunteers launched a political organization called Brand New Congress with the goal of advancing Sanders's platform by recruiting progressive candidates to run for office. Four months later, Sanders founded another organization, Our Revolution, that focused on increasing voters' understanding of and involvement in the political process.

After Clinton lost the November 2016 presidential election to Republican candidate Donald Trump—a billionaire real-estate developer and television personality—an increasing number of Democrats decided that the moderate approach she adopted in her campaign was no longer relevant or effective. Concerned that Trump would pursue policies that favored large corporations and wealthy donors at the expense of working people and families, they argued that a more radical approach was needed. Some critics embraced democratic socialism as an alternative to modern American capitalism, which they considered responsible for growing economic inequality and other problems.

Democratic socialists argue that capitalism is "fundamentally undemocratic," according to Maria Svart, national director of the Democratic Socialists of America (DSA), because free-market forces tend to benefit a few wealthy business owners rather than serving the public good. DSA supporters propose restructuring the U.S. government and economy in fundamental ways to limit the power of corporations, empower working people, and create what they describe as a more just and equitable society. "When it comes right down to it, we believe people need to be able to live a dignified life," Svart stated. "There are certain things that should not be left up to the market" (Kurtzleben and Malone 2018). As a starting point, democratic socialists promoted such initiatives as the Medicare for All public health program and the Fight for $15 minimum wage campaign.

Although these initiatives had seemed extreme when Sanders first discussed them in his 2016 campaign, they gained greater mainstream acceptance following Trump's election. "Today, virtually all of those ideas are supported by a majority of the American people," Sanders said in 2019. "And they are ideas that Democratic candidates from school board to presidential candidates are running on today" (Krieg 2019). Sanders's campaign also served as a catalyst for growth for the DSA, which saw its national membership increase from around 5,000 when he launched his presidential bid to more than 50,000 in 2018 (Relman 2019).

Democratic socialism held particular appeal for millennials, who entered the job market just as the U.S. economy entered the Great Recession. As their wages stagnated, they watched the costs of education, housing, and health care skyrocket. Like Ocasio-Cortez, many young people lived from paycheck to paycheck and worried about the future. "Thanks to the economic downturn of 2008, which turned the millennial generation in a significant way to the left, it made them much more open to the idea of socialism," said Maurice Isserman, a charter member of the DSA (Kurtzleben and Malone 2018). According to Gallup polls, support for capitalism among Americans between the ages of 18 and 29 declined from 68 percent in 2010 to 45 percent in 2018 (Krieg 2019). Meanwhile, around one-third of young voters approved of the concept of socialism (Levitz 2019).

Although many of the progressive policy proposals favored by the DSA garner widespread support, many older Americans associate socialism with failed Cold War–era governments and view young democratic socialists with suspicion. In fact, conservative commentators frequently describe proposals to expand worker rights and protections as socialist in order to foment opposition to them. President Trump appealed to anti-socialist mistrust in his 2019 State of the Union address. "We are alarmed by new calls to adopt socialism in our country," he said. "America was founded on liberty and independence—not government coercion, domination, and control. We are born free, and we will stay free. Tonight, we renew our resolve that America will never be a socialist country" (Trump 2019).

Some Democrats expressed concern that associating the party with socialist ideas might alienate moderate voters. For Ocasio-Cortez, however, Sanders's platform and democratic socialism had strong resonance. "I believe that in a modern, moral, and wealthy society, no person in America should be too poor to live," she stated. "What that means to me is health care as a human right. It means that every child, no matter where you are born, should have access to a college or trade school education if they so choose it. And, you know, I think that no person should be homeless if we can have public structures and public policy to allow for people to have homes and food and lead a dignified life in the United States" (Clifford 2018).

BERNIE SANDERS

Bernard ("Bernie") Sanders was born to a Jewish family in Brooklyn, New York, on September 8, 1941. During his college years at the University of Chicago, he became politically active in the antiwar and civil rights movements of the 1960s, participating in sit-in protests and attending the 1963 March on Washington. He eventually settled in Vermont and, after several unsuccessful attempts, launched a career in politics by being elected mayor of Burlington in 1981. Nine years later, Vermont voters sent Sanders to the U.S. Congress, where he served eight terms in the House of Representatives before winning election to the Senate in 2006.

Although he is considered an Independent, Sanders caucuses with the Democratic Party. He is a founding member of the Congressional Progressive Caucus, which represents the liberal left wing of the Democratic Party, and often describes himself as a democratic socialist. "What democratic socialism means to me is having, in a civilized society, the understanding that we can make sure that all of our people live in security and in dignity," Sanders explained. "To me, when I talk about democratic socialism, what I talk about are human rights and economic rights" (Haltiwanger 2019). During his tenure in Congress, Sanders gained a reputation for opposing tax cuts that favored wealthy individuals and corporations and supporting the expansion of social-welfare programs that benefited poor and working-class people.

Although unsuccessful, Sanders's 2016 presidential campaign attracted enthusiastic support from liberal voters—particularly young people—and made him an influential voice in progressive politics. In February 2019, Sanders announced his intention to seek the Democratic presidential nomination once again in 2020.

FURTHER READING

Alter, Charlotte. 2019. "'Change Is Closer Than We Think': Inside Alexandria Ocasio-Cortez's Unlikely Rise." *Time*, March 21, 2019. http://time.com/longform/alexandria-ocasio-cortez-profile/.

Cadigan, Hilary. 2018. "Alexandria Ocasio-Cortez Learned Her Most Important Lessons from Restaurants." *Bon Appetit*, November 7, 2018. https://www.yahoo.com/lifestyle/alexandria-ocasio-cortez-learned-her-141500873.html.

Clifford, Catherine. 2018. "Young Political Star Ocasio-Cortez: In a Moral, Wealthy Society, 'No Person in America Should Be Too Poor to Live.'" CNBC, June 29, 2018. https://www.cnbc.com/2018/06/29/alexandria-ocasio-cortez-talks-poverty-in-the-us-with-steven-colbert.html.

Griffith, Keith. 2018. "I Grew Up between Two Worlds." *Daily Mail*, July 2, 2018. https://www.dailymail.co.uk/news/article-5908173/Bronx-candidate-Alexandria-Ocasio-Cortez-blasts-questions-working-class-roots.html.

Haltiwanger, John. 2019. "Here's the Difference between a 'Socialist' and a 'Democratic Socialist.'" *Business Insider*, February 25, 2019. https://www.businessinsider.com/difference-between-socialist-and-democratic-socialist-2018-6.

Kane, Paul, and Philip Rucker. 2015. "An Unlikely Contender, Sanders Takes on 'Billionaire Class' in 2016 Bid." *The Washington Post*, April 29, 2015. https://www.washingtonpost.com/politics/sanders-takes-on-billionaire-class-in-launching-2016-bid-against-clinton/2015/04/30/4849fe32-ef3a-11e4-a55f-38924fca94f9_story.html?utm_term=.731c80c3c3a1.

Krieg, Gregory. 2019. "Four Years after Bernie Sanders' 2016 Success, Young Democratic Socialists Go Mainstream." CNN, March 13, 2019. https://www.cnn.com/2019/03/13/politics/democratic-socialists-bernie-sanders-2020/index.html.

Kurtzleben, Danielle, and Kenny Malone. 2018. "What You Need to Know about the Democratic Socialists of America." NPR, July 26, 2018. https://www.npr.org/2018/07/26/630960719/what-you-need-to-know-about-the-democratic-socialists-of-america.

Levitz, Eric. 2019. "Bernie Sanders: 'Democratic Socialist' Is Just a Synonym for New Deal Liberal." *New York Magazine*, April 23, 2019. http://nymag.com/intelligencer/2019/04/bernie-sanders-democratic-socialism-new-deal-liberalism-cnn-town-hall.html.

Morris, Alex. 2019. "Alexandria Ocasio-Cortez Wants the Country to Think Big." *Rolling Stone*, February 27, 2019. https://www.rollingstone.com/politics/politics-features/alexandria-ocasio-cortez-congress-interview-797214/.

National Hispanic Institute. 2017. "Alexandria Ocasio-Cortez Named 2017 NHI Person of the Year." *NHI Magazine*, December 31, 2017. http://www.nhimagazine.com/2017/12/31/alexandria-ocasio-cortez-named-2017-nhi-person-year/.

Relman, Eliza. 2019. "The Truth about Alexandria Ocasio-Cortez." *Insider*, January 6, 2019. https://www.thisisinsider.com/alexandria-ocasio-cortez-biography-2019-1.

Remnick, David. 2018. "Alexandria Ocasio-Cortez's Historic Win and the Future of the Democratic Party." *The New Yorker,* July 16, 2018. https://www.newyorker.com/magazine/2018/07/23/alexandria-ocasio-cortezs-historic-win-and-the-future-of-the-democratic-party.

Trump, Donald J. 2019. "Remarks by President Trump in State of the Union Address." The White House, February 5, 2019. https://www.whitehouse.gov/briefings-statements/remarks-president-trump-state-union-address-2/.

Chapter 4

POLITICAL AWAKENING

Times of great challenge can also bring out the best in people. . . . Even though things are hitting the fan right now, we're seeing people activate and educate themselves. (Hayes 2019)

Although Alexandria Ocasio-Cortez felt disappointed when her preferred candidate, Bernie Sanders, failed to claim the 2016 Democratic presidential nomination, she felt confident that Democratic nominee Hillary Clinton would defeat Republican nominee Donald Trump in the general election and become the first female president of the United States. In the weeks before American voters cast their ballots on November 8, pollsters and pundits agreed that Clinton was the heavy favorite. But although Clinton won the popular vote, Trump pulled out a narrow electoral college victory. Ocasio-Cortez and other progressives were shocked by the results, which contributed to widespread feelings of grief, outrage, and disillusionment with the American political system.

Ocasio-Cortez had supported Sanders's campaign because she shared his concerns about growing economic inequality, which made it difficult for young people in her generation to achieve a comfortable, middle-class lifestyle. She worried that Trump and the Republican-controlled Congress would exacerbate the divide between rich and poor in America by cutting taxes for large corporations and wealthy donors and reducing federal spending on health care and social welfare programs. In addition, since Trump had made controversial and insulting comments about women, racial and ethnic minorities, immigrants, Muslims, and LGBTQ individuals during his campaign, she worried that his administration would roll back civil rights protections for these groups and implement policies that would prove detrimental to their welfare.

Millions of people on the left side of the political spectrum shared Ocasio-Cortez's concerns. Many liberals responded to Trump's election by becoming more politically active and organizing grassroots opposition to the new president's policies. An early manifestation of this surge in political energy came in January 2017, immediately following Trump's inauguration, when an estimated five million protesters around the world participated in the Women's March. The anti-Trump resistance movement also led to the formation of dozens of progressive political groups—such as Indivisible, Swing Left, and Justice Democrats—that worked to disrupt Trump's agenda, put pressure on Republican representatives, and register Democratic voters. Across the country, liberal activists made phone calls, sent e-mails, attended protest marches and rallies, picketed outside representatives' offices, and packed town hall meetings to make their voices heard.

THE FLINT WATER CRISIS

Still reeling from the election results and feeling a strong urge to increase her political involvement, Ocasio-Cortez joined some friends on a cross-country road trip in late 2016. They planned to participate in demonstrations calling for environmental justice in communities where low-income, minority residents were fighting against powerful corporate and government interests for access to clean drinking water. Their first stop was Flint, Michigan, a struggling industrial city of around 100,000 residents—more than half of whom are African American—with a median annual household income of approximately

$25,000. Once a hub of automobile manufacturing, Flint experienced a long economic decline beginning in the 1980s, and in 2011 the State of Michigan placed the city in financial receivership.

In 2014, as a cost-cutting measure, state emergency managers changed the source of Flint's drinking water supply from the city of Detroit's water-treatment facilities to the Flint River. Officials failed to treat the river water with an anti-corrosive agent, however, which resulted in lead leaching from the city's older water mains and residential water pipes. Although Flint residents complained about foul-smelling, discolored drinking water—and tests conducted by the U.S. Environmental Protection Agency and independent organizations found dangerous levels of lead in some homes—city and state officials repeatedly claimed that the water was safe. Finally, in 2016, Republican governor Rick Snyder issued a disaster declaration, and state and federal agencies began distributing faucet filters and bottled water to Flint residents. By this time, thousands of Flint children had been exposed to unsafe levels of lead, which can damage developing brains. Fifteen local and state officials eventually faced criminal charges for their mishandling of the Flint water crisis.

Visiting Flint and speaking with residents affected by the water crisis had a profound impact on Ocasio-Cortez. "Flint plays a very important role in the start of my story," she noted (Roth 2018). Ocasio-Cortez recalled spending hours in a Flint diner discussing the various factors that had caused the crisis and allowed government officials to deny or ignore it for so long. She concluded that the race and socioeconomic status of Flint's population made them a low priority for the politicians elected to represent their interests. She became convinced that the influence of money in politics had left the people powerless. "There was no real clear answer" as to why the crisis happened, Ocasio-Cortez stated, "except one thing: that there were too many people who put themselves, who put corporations, who put lobbyist influence, who put money ahead of the lives of everyday people here in Flint" (Roth 2018).

THE STANDING ROCK PROTESTS

Ocasio-Cortez and her friends left Michigan and continued driving west to the Standing Rock Indian Reservation, which straddles the border between North Dakota and South Dakota. In early 2016, a natural gas exploration and development company called Energy Transfer Partners received approval to build a 1,200-mile underground oil pipeline from the Bakken oil fields in North Dakota to distribution facilities in Illinois. This project, known as the Dakota Access Pipeline (DAPL), would extend beneath Lake Oahe near the northeast corner of the Standing Rock Reservation and pass below the Missouri and Mississippi Rivers. Members of the Standing Rock Sioux Tribe expressed concerns about the potential for oil spills from the DAPL to contaminate their drinking water supplies and destroy their sacred lands. They argued that the U.S. Army Corps of Engineers had approved the project without sufficient review of its environmental impact and filed lawsuits to block construction. Company representatives claimed that the pipeline construction involved private property rather than reservation land and did not pose a threat to the watershed.

In April 2016, a group of Native American activists led by Lakota elder LaDonna Brave Bull Allard established a camp for organized, peaceful resistance to the DAPL. Over the next few months, the Standing Rock protests attracted support from indigenous rights activists and environmental justice advocates around the world. Online supporters sent millions of dollars in cash and supplies to aid the "water protectors," while thousands of people traveled to the reservation to join the protests. Many observers expressed outrage when law enforcement and private security personnel used what they considered unnecessarily aggressive and violent tactics against the demonstrators. Standing Rock activists produced video footage showing officers dressed in riot gear and armed with military equipment using attack dogs, tear gas, rubber bullets, and water cannons against unarmed protesters.

Ocasio-Cortez spent several weeks living at the Standing Rock camp and participating in the anti-DAPL protests in late 2016. She described the experience as a "tipping point" that launched her political awakening. "I saw how all of the people there—particularly the Native people and the Lakota Sioux—were putting their whole lives and everything that they had on the line for the protection of their community," she recalled. "I saw how a corporation had literally militarized itself against the American people, and I just felt like we were at a point where we couldn't afford to ignore politics anymore. We couldn't afford to write off our collective power in self-governance anymore out of cynicism" (Paiella 2018).

As the Standing Rock protests garnered international media attention, President Barack Obama issued an executive order denying Energy Transfer Partners an easement to run the DAPL beneath the Missouri River until a full environmental impact assessment could be completed. Shortly after taking office in January 2017, however, Trump reversed the order and allowed construction to continue. Law enforcement cleared the camps of protesters in February, and two months later the DAPL became operational, transporting 500,000 barrels of oil per day.

DECIDING TO RUN FOR OFFICE

Ocasio-Cortez described her post–election road trip as a "transformational" experience. "I think the me that walked out of that," she noted, "was more galvanized and more open to taking risks." Ocasio-Cortez claimed that visiting Flint and Standing Rock helped her "connect a lot of different dots" between corporate money, political power, and government inaction in the face of environmental degradation and health threats affecting marginalized populations (Alter 2019). She learned that ordinary, working-class people faced similar problems in her hometown and in cities all over the United States. "A Bronx public high school tested with lead in their water 16 times higher than Flint. And they tried to tell us that the struggle of the Bronx is different than the struggle of Flint, that it's different than the struggle of Standing Rock," Ocasio-Cortez stated. "What we do to Flint is what we do to the Bronx, is what we do to Standing Rock, is what we do to Baltimore, is what we do to Kansas City, is what we do to St. Louis. How we treat Flint is how we treat the nation" (Roth 2018).

As she drove back to the Bronx from North Dakota, Ocasio-Cortez received a phone call from Brand New Congress (BNC)—the political action group formed by Sanders supporters to recruit progressive candidates to run for office. BNC's original goal involved running a full slate of 435 crowd-sourced candidates—mostly young people, women, people of color, working-class people, and newcomers without political connections—to challenge established incumbent politicians from both parties and replace the entire membership of the U.S. House of Representatives. "We don't care about party. We just want to get stuff done," said BNC organizer Isra Allison. "If we elect working people, working people can have representation in Congress" (Lears 2019).

BNC put out calls for candidates on social media and through progressive news sources. The group received nearly 11,000 applications on its website, promoting community leaders with varying backgrounds and qualifications from congressional districts all across the country. One application, submitted by New York City resident Gabriel Ocasio-Cortez, endorsed his older sister, Alexandria, presenting her as a passionate young Latina activist who had earned an economics degree but worked as a waitress to help support her family. BNC staff members found the nomination interesting and placed it in a pile of potential candidates to contact. "We looked at the brother telling the story of a sister who wasn't a giant nonprofit executive, she didn't go work on the Hill for 10 years," recalled BNC organizer Alexandra Rojas. "She was someone who watched her family struggle through the financial crisis" (Alter 2019).

Although Ocasio-Cortez knew her brother had submitted her name, she was surprised to hear from BNC. During the initial phone call, Allison told Ocasio-Cortez that the group was seeking candidates who supported Sanders's progressive ideas, such as Medicare for All, and would agree to forego all corporate campaign funding. "She told me what BNC was about," Ocasio-Cortez remembered. "I was just, like, 'OK, I'm listening.' By that time, they had policy plans, and Sanders was the political shorthand" (Remnick 2018). Ocasio-Cortez agreed to submit some follow-up materials, including a video of her 2011 King Day speech at Boston University and a statement outlining what she had learned by working in the food-service industry.

Even as she discussed the possibility, Ocasio-Cortez had serious doubts about running for Congress. She recognized that her youth, inexperience, and modest financial means presented major obstacles to a successful political campaign. "I never really saw myself running on my own. I counted out that possibility because I felt that possibility had counted out me," she explained. "I felt like the only way to effectively run for office is if you had access to a lot of wealth, high social influence, a lot of high dynastic power, and I knew that I didn't have any of those things" (Paiella 2018). Some of Ocasio-Cortez's doubts stemmed from her disillusionment with the American political system. "I wasn't sure if our democracy and its electoral politics were really salvageable in the interests of working-class people," she acknowledged (Stuart 2018).

Over the next few weeks, as Ocasio-Cortez reflected on her experiences in Flint and in the "crucible of activism" at Standing Rock (Solnit 2019), she felt a responsibility to serve the interests of underrepresented groups in the Bronx and elsewhere. "That experience was very personally important and transformative, and I kind of left feeling like I had to do more, and I didn't know what that was," she recalled. "When I got that call, I just felt like, 'OK, the universe is telling me something, so I'm going to listen'" (Feller 2018). Ocasio-Cortez began to view her political liabilities as potential strengths, and she agreed to run for Congress in New York's Fourteenth Congressional District. "In order for us to change course, and change the future, it's going to take people who haven't typically been seen or thought of as a typical candidate," she noted. "And it's going to take strategies and resources that haven't been used before. It's going to take people that reject big money and lobbyist influence to help charge this path forward" (Caraballo 2018).

In the meantime, several leaders of BNC split off to form another progressive political organization, Justice Democrats. When BNC's initial strategy of launching and supporting 435 congressional campaigns turned out to be unrealistic, Justice Democrats stepped in with a more modest approach. The organization decided to concentrate its resources behind twelve working-class candidates without political experience to mount primary challenges against established, incumbent Democrats with centrist views. By contesting Democratic primaries, Justice Democrats hoped to shift the party's platform leftward and encourage mainstream Democrats to support progressive policies designed to help working people, such as increasing the federal minimum wage. Trump's electoral victory over Clinton convinced progressive activists that the party needed to radically alter its approach. "I came to realize Democrats are never going to learn," said Justice Democrats cofounder Cenk Uygur, "and that the only way to make a difference is to defeat the corrupt corporate Democrats" (Freedlander 2019). Ocasio-Cortez thus became one of the dozen outsiders selected by Justice Democrats to mount a populist campaign attacking an established Democrat from the left.

GABRIEL OCASIO-CORTEZ

Alexandria Ocasio-Cortez may never have launched her congressional campaign without a push from her younger brother, Gabriel. He submitted an application on her behalf to Brand New Congress, a political action committee that recruited progressive candidates to challenge established incumbents in the 2018 midterm elections, and provided unwavering support throughout her campaign. When Alexandria took the oath of office to serve as a member of the 116th U.S. Congress, her brother stood by her side. Afterward, Gabriel described himself on Twitter as "the proudest Brother in the World" (Igoe 2019).

Gabriel was born in the Bronx on November 25, 1991. He and Alexandria were very close growing up and shared the experience of attending public school in suburban Yorktown Heights. Inspired by his own struggles to overcome single-sided deafness and tinnitus, Gabriel went on to earn a degree in art psychotherapy from Long Island University. Like his sister, he often worked multiple jobs to help support the family. While serving as a real-estate agent and consultant in Armonk, New York, he also pursued his creative passions as a painter, songwriter, musician, and singer. In 2019, Gabriel Ocasio-Cortez (known as GOC) launched his own YouTube channel and blog series.

FURTHER READING

Alter, Charlotte. 2019. "'Change Is Closer Than We Think': Inside Alexandria Ocasio-Cortez's Unlikely Rise." *Time*, March 21, 2019. http://time.com/longform/alexandria-ocasio-cortez-profile/.

Caraballo, Ecleen Luzmila. 2018. "'We Have to Apply Pressure': Alexandria Ocasio-Cortez Is Done with the Democratic Status Quo."

Jezebel, June 26, 2018. https://theslot.jezebel.com/we-have-to-apply-pressure-alexandria-ocasio-cortez-is-1827143440.

Feller, Madison. 2018. "Alexandria Ocasio-Cortez Knows She Can't Save America All by Herself." *Elle*, July 16, 2018. https://www.elle.com/culture/career-politics/a22118408/alexandria-ocasio-cortez-interview/.

Freedlander, David. 2019. "There Is Going to Be a War within the Party. We Are Going to Lean into It." Politico, February 4, 2019. https://www.politico.com/magazine/story/2019/02/04/the-insurgents-behind-alexandria-ocasio-cortez-224542.

Hayes, Christal. 2019. "Alexandria Ocasio-Cortez Says She Could Have Been a Teacher If It Wasn't for Trump." *USA Today*, February 22, 2019. https://www.usatoday.com/story/news/politics/2019/02/22/alexandria-ocasio-cortez-said-she-might-teaching-if-not-trump/2952850002/.

Igoe, Katherine J. 2019. "Who Is Alexandria Ocasio-Cortez's Brother Gabriel? He's an Artist and Musician." *Marie Claire*, February 8, 2019. https://www.marieclaire.com/politics/a26251021/alexandria-ocasio-cortez-brother-gabriel/.

Lears, Rachel. 2019. *Knock Down the House* [documentary film]. Netflix. New York: Jubilee Films.

Paiella, Gabriella. 2018. "The 28-Year-Old at the Center of One of This Year's Most Exciting Primaries." *New York Magazine*, June 25, 2018. https://www.thecut.com/2018/06/alexandria-ocasio-cortez-interview.html.

Remnick, David. 2018. "Alexandria Ocasio-Cortez's Historic Win and the Future of the Democratic Party." *The New Yorker*, July 16, 2018. https://www.newyorker.com/magazine/2018/07/23/alexandria-ocasio-cortezs-historic-win-and-the-future-of-the-democratic-party.

Roth, Andrew. 2018. "El-Sayed, Ocasio-Cortez Discuss Personal Ties to Flint during Rally." *Flint Beat*, August 14, 2018. http://flintbeat.com/el-sayed-ocasio-cortez-discuss-personal-ties-to-flint-during-rally/.

Solnit, Rebecca. 2019. "Standing Rock Inspired Ocasio-Cortez to Run. That's the Power of Protest." *Guardian*, January 14, 2019.

https://www.theguardian.com/commentisfree/2019/jan/14/standing-rock-ocasio-cortez-protest-climate-activism.

Stuart, Tessa. 2018. "Alexandria Ocasio-Cortez: 'I Lean into the Misconceptions.'" *Rolling Stone*, October 8, 2018. https://www.rollingstone.com/politics/politics-features/alexandria-ocasio-cortez-interview-2-732173/.

Chapter 5

DEMOCRATIC PRIMARY CAMPAIGN

Anyone who wants to keep their job in New York City would never dream of challenging Joe Crowley. It has to come from outside of Queens, it has to come from someone who's new on the political scene . . . that they can't offer a job or pressure in another way, and it has to be someone who represents our community in more ways than one. Basically, an insurgent, outside, grassroots candidate that's a woman of color from the Bronx. (Lears 2019)

When she decided to run for Congress, Alexandria Ocasio-Cortez knew that her campaign faced extremely long odds of success. As an unknown political outsider with limited resources, she seemed unlikely to mount a serious challenge against Representative Joseph Crowley in the Democratic primary for New York's Fourteenth Congressional District. Crowley was a ten-term incumbent who first took office in 1999, when Ocasio-Cortez was 10 years old, and eventually rose to the powerful position of chair of the House Democratic Caucus. He thus became the legislative body's fourth-highest ranking Democrat and a leading candidate to succeed Nancy Pelosi (D-CA) as speaker of the House.

Born in Queens in 1962, Crowley earned a degree in political science from Queens College in 1985. Two years later, he launched a career in politics by winning election to the New York State Assembly. During his decade in the state legislature, Crowley steadily gained influence within New York City's Democratic political "machine," which is based on longstanding relationships between politicians and local constituency groups. "He was an old-school power broker, someone who commanded a party organization that could make loyal soldiers into elected officeholders," David Freedlander wrote in Politico. "He was someone who anyone who wanted to be governor, senator, mayor, or speaker of the City Council had to pay tribute to" (Freedlander 2019a).

Crowley's position within the party establishment played a role in his ascension to the U.S. Congress. Representative Thomas Manton (1932–2006), who had held the seat since 1985, initially sought reelection in 1998 but withdrew from the race at the last minute. As head of the Queens County Democratic Party, Manton handpicked Crowley, his friend and protégé, to replace him on the ballot. Since it was too late for other candidates to mount a primary challenge, Crowley prevailed easily in the heavily Democratic district.

The New York Times criticized the maneuver at the time, asserting that Manton had only filed for reelection in order to select his own replacement. Ocasio-Cortez contended that the controversial circumstances surrounding his initial candidacy cast a shadow over Crowley's subsequent two decades in office. "He wasn't democratically elected," she said. "He didn't democratically win a primary. That is how we've had such unrepresentative representation of our district for so long" (Joyce 2018). Crowley went on to assume Manton's position as head of the Democratic Party in the borough following his mentor's death, and he became known as the "King of Queens" for the power he exerted over New York City politics.

Given Crowley's prominence, most observers considered it pointless to challenge him. In fact, Crowley had not faced competition in a Democratic primary for fourteen years prior to Ocasio-Cortez joining the race in 2018. "Anybody who knew anything about politics in New York City told me not to do this," Ocasio-Cortez recalled. "[They said] (a) you're wasting your time, (b) it's pointless, and (c) you'll never have a career in New York City politics ever again if you do this"

(Lipsitz 2018). Many observers demanded to know why, as a political newcomer, Ocasio-Cortez felt she was qualified to challenge such an established lawmaker. "The fundamental question, in the beginning, is, 'Why you?'" she acknowledged. "The reason 'why' was because nobody else would. So literally anybody could, right? Because the alternative is no one" (Lears 2019).

Ocasio-Cortez also noted that the demographics of New York City's Fourteenth District had changed considerably during the two decades Crowley had been in office, and especially since the district's borders were redrawn following the 2010 census. By 2018, it ranked among the most racially and ethnically diverse areas in the United States, with over one hundred languages spoken within its boundaries. Some critics questioned whether Crowley, as a white man of Irish descent, was the most appropriate person to represent a district whose population had become half Hispanic and less than 20 percent white. "We're a district that covers the Bronx and Queens and Rikers Island," Ocasio-Cortez explained (Joyce 2018). "A community that is 70 percent people of color has never had a person of color represent them in American history" (Chávez and Grim 2018).

WAGING A GRASSROOTS CAMPAIGN

Prior to launching her campaign, Ocasio-Cortez received training from Brand New Congress and Justice Democrats to help her develop policy positions, media strategy, and debate tactics. She also learned about the Federal Election Commission rules for collecting signatures, filing paperwork, and raising money to run for office. Since her opponent served as head of the Democratic Party for the district, Ocasio-Cortez and her advisers understood that they had to be meticulous to avoid giving Crowley's appointees an excuse for keeping her name off the ballot. Realizing that petitions could be disallowed for minor discrepancies, they submitted 10,000 signatures instead of the required 1,250 (Lears 2019). Ocasio-Cortez was thrilled when the elections board approved her petition and her candidacy became official.

When Ocasio-Cortez launched her campaign in May 2017, she knew that her opponent held a major financial advantage. As an entrenched incumbent and party boss, Crowley was a prolific fundraiser with extensive contacts in the business community. His campaign committee took in more than $3 million for the 2017–2018 campaign cycle, with most of it coming in the form of large contributions from individual donors or political action committees (PACs) representing the interests of luxury real-estate developers and Wall Street investment banks. Ocasio-Cortez, on the other hand, refused to accept campaign funding from corporate PACs. She asserted that doing so made politicians represent wealthy business interests rather than constituent concerns. Her campaign committee only raised about $200,000 before the primary election, with the majority coming in the form of small donations ($22, on average) from individual donors. "This race is about people versus money," she stated. "We've got people. They've got money" (Steiger 2018).

The funding discrepancy influenced many aspects of Ocasio-Cortez's campaign strategy. She continued working as a bartender and server at Flats Fix for the first nine months of her campaign. She kept a change of clothes and a stack of campaign flyers in a paper grocery sack tucked behind the bar, and she spent a few hours canvassing after her shift ended. Waleed Shahid, an organizer with Justice Democrats, recalled that Ocasio-Cortez's work schedule often made it difficult to schedule meetings and appearances. "I would get so frustrated with her," he related. "'You can't do this full-time bartending thing and run for Congress!' And she would say, 'What do you want me to do? I have to work'" (Freedlander 2019b).

With a group of volunteers that included friends and family members as well as campaign strategists and political organizers from Brand New Congress, Justice Democrats, and local progressive groups, Ocasio-Cortez employed a grassroots, insurgent approach. She rented a small office in Queens for a campaign headquarters and established an informal, leaderless organization modeled after the Standing Rock protests. Reflecting the low-budget nature and flexible structure of the campaign, volunteer staff members wrote their job titles on pieces of paper and stuck them to their desks.

Ocasio-Cortez knew she could not compete with Crowley by sending out glossy mailers or purchasing airtime for television ads, so she tried to forge a personal connection with as many residents of the Fourteenth District as possible. During the year-long campaign, she and her volunteers knocked on 120,000 doors, made 170,000 phone calls, and sent out 120,000 text messages (Remnick 2018). Recognizing her district's diversity, Ocasio-Cortez had campaign workers who were able to speak with voters in six languages: English, Spanish, Albanian, Arabic, Bengali, and Mandarin.

Ocasio-Cortez met with constituents in living rooms, church basements, neighborhood parks, and community centers. Her goal was to generate excitement and increase turnout among voters who had not previously shown much interest in primaries, such as young people and people of color. "The Democratic Party takes working-class communities for granted, they take people of color for granted," Ocasio-Cortez asserted, "and they just assume that we're going to turn out no matter how bland or half-stepping these proposals are" (Goldmacher and Martin 2018).

To position herself as a representative of working-class interests, Ocasio-Cortez also worked with the creative firm Tandem to design visually striking, bilingual campaign posters inspired by "revolutionary posters and visuals from the past," such as those used by Latino labor activists Cesar Chavez and Dolores Huerta. "That was the closest representation to a populist, social-minded, justice-inclined, inspirational campaign that was about positivity and taking back the power," Tandem cofounder Scott Starrett explained (Budds 2018). The posters featured a portrait of Ocasio-Cortez looking off into the distance, her name in capital letters with Spanish-style exclamation points on both sides, and bold background colors, including purple, blue, and rainbow hues.

PROMOTING PROGRESSIVE IDEAS

Ocasio-Cortez's visual brand matched the progressive ideas she promoted in her democratic socialist platform. Describing income inequality as the most pressing issue facing the nation, she called for a political revolution to elevate the interests of working-class Americans above those of millionaires and multinational corporations. "Many members of Congress were born into wealth, or they grew up around it," Ocasio-Cortez said, noting that the median net worth of federal legislators was five times that of an average American household. "How can you legislate a better life for working people if you've never been a working person?" (Cadigan 2018).

Ocasio-Cortez's platform included many of the same planks as Bernie Sanders's populist presidential campaign, such as expanding the federal Medicare program to provide health coverage to all Americans, establishing a $15 minimum wage, and increasing access to higher education through tuition-free public college. She also expressed support for stronger gun control measures and proposed ending the cash-bail system, which she said disproportionately harms low-income and minority populations and contributes to the problem of mass incarceration. Ocasio-Cortez also campaigned on promises to combat global climate change, champion equal rights for women and LGBTQ individuals, support hurricane recovery in Puerto Rico, and abolish the U.S. Immigration and Customs Enforcement Agency (ICE), which she claimed violated the human rights of immigrants.

Ocasio-Cortez's ambitious platform led some critics to call her a socialist—a term that conjured up negative images of repressive regimes in the minds of some voters. The candidate's mother, Blanca, explained how her daughter's democratic socialist ideology differed from traditional socialism. "She wasn't raised to be a socialist. That's not how Puerto Ricans are. That's not what we do. Socialists are in Cuba or Venezuela. Besides, anyone who tries to help little people like me is branded a socialist," she stated. "She's a democratic socialist, and it's very different. They focus on working people's needs. They're not about the rich or big corporations. Democratic socialists are about what Democrats were supposed to be about, but Democrats are not doing a good enough job" (Lambiet 2019).

Although Ocasio-Cortez belonged to the Democratic Socialists of America, she resisted efforts to label her political ideology and instead focused on her goals and beliefs. "It's easy to generate fear around an idea or around an -ism when you don't provide any substance to it," she said. "I believe that every American should have stable, dignified housing; health care; education—that the most very basic needs to sustain modern life should be guaranteed in a moral society. You can call that whatever you want" (Paiella 2018).

Ocasio-Cortez made extensive use of social media to spread her message to voters. She found Twitter particularly valuable in allowing her to bypass the traditional news media, communicate directly with community members, and build relationships with potential supporters. Twitter also provided a space where she could refine her campaign platform and polish her pitch to voters. "It was literally just through tweeting and getting that feedback and learning through commentary and testing messages," she recalled. "Because every time you tweet something how it performs is basically like an A/B test [a randomized comparison of two alternatives]" (Relman 2019). Over the course of her primary campaign, Ocasio-Cortez watched as her number of Twitter followers increased from fewer than 300 to more than 60,000. At one point, she tweeted a photograph of the shoes she wore while canvassing, which were soaking wet and falling apart, with the caption "Respect the hustle" (Remnick 2018).

About a month before primary day, Ocasio-Cortez released a two-minute campaign video on social media called "The Courage to Change." Shot in her Bronx neighborhood by democratic socialist filmmakers Naomi Burton and Nick Hayes of the Detroit-based company Means of Production, the video follows the candidate from her modest apartment to her local bodega and to a nearby subway platform. In a voiceover narrative, Ocasio-Cortez describes her working-class background and commitment to serving the community. She goes on to discuss how economic inequality has led to the gentrification of neighborhoods and other changes that have benefited the wealthy and harmed ordinary New Yorkers. "Women like me aren't supposed to run for office," she says in the voiceover. "But after 20 years of the same representation, we have to ask: Who has New York been changing for? Every day gets harder for working families like mine to get by. The rent gets higher, health care covers less, and our income stays the same. It's clear that these changes haven't been for us."

Ocasio-Cortez goes on to characterize Crowley as a career politician who has lost touch with his constituents and does not understand their struggles. "It's time we acknowledge that not all Democrats are the same," she says. "That a Democrat who takes corporate money, profits off foreclosure, doesn't live here, doesn't send his kids to our schools, doesn't drink our water or breathe our air, cannot possibly represent us. . . . A New York for the many is possible. It's time for one of us" (Ocasio-Cortez 2018). Ocasio-Cortez noted that she did not utilize the services of media consultants in producing the video. Instead, she wrote the script herself and coordinated the shoot with volunteers. It immediately went viral on social media, receiving 300,000 views on the day it was released and eventually tallying 4 million. The popularity of the campaign video led to a surge in donations, hundreds of new volunteers, a few high-profile endorsements, and national media attention.

SQUARING OFF IN CANDIDATE DEBATES

For much of the primary campaign, Ocasio-Cortez and her supporters expected to get 30 percent of the vote at best. A poll conducted in January showed Crowley with a huge lead, although it also suggested that his name recognition and approval ratings were fairly low for an established incumbent. Through the late winter and early spring, the Crowley campaign barely seemed to acknowledge Ocasio-Cortez's primary challenge. "Sexism, I think . . . informed a lot of the way this political machine reacted to me, and I used it to my advantage," she noted. "'She's uninformed, she's young, she's naive, she's nothing to worry about'—I was ignored for 99.9 percent of my campaign, and I liked it that way" (Stuart 2018).

Ocasio-Cortez received some early indications that her campaign may have gotten Crowley's attention. She celebrated when it appeared that her opponent shifted his positions leftward on such issues as Medicare for All and the Fight for $15 in response to her platform. Nevertheless, her campaign managers sometimes felt bad about raising the hopes of supporters, given the slim chance of Ocasio-Cortez prevailing in the primary. "We would go to these fundraisers in the Bronx, and there would be ex-cops in the room and they would have tears in their eyes," Shahid remembered. "I had just come off the Bernie [Sanders] campaign and here AOC was, she was so . . . inspiring and so charismatic that grown men are crying, and I would think to myself, 'We just have no chance here. Everyone is going to be so disappointed!'" (Freedlander 2019b).

Ocasio-Cortez managed to maintain her optimism, however, and kept knocking on doors, pushing her platform, and connecting with voters. "Even when things looked their worst—like in January when it was just me and my partner in our apartment and I was bartending full-time while challenging one of the most powerful members of Congress—never did I feel like I didn't have a shot," she recalled. "Because I'm an organizer. I'm on the ground. I know my community. We acknowledge that all this [stuff] is stacked up against us, but we don't get to give up. We don't have the luxury" (Cadigan 2018).

By May 2018, it became clear that Ocasio-Cortez's efforts had begun to pay off. As her campaign generated buzz on the New York City streets and on social media, both the national press and her heavily favored opponent took notice. During the last six weeks before the election, the Crowley campaign sprang into action, producing television ads and blanketing the district with mailers touting the incumbent's staunch opposition to the Trump administration's policies. Some neighborhoods reportedly received a dozen pieces of Crowley campaign literature, which Ocasio-Cortez claimed inadvertently raised awareness of her insurgent bid. "It's funny," she said. "A lot of people find our campaign because he comes out for the first time and they're like 'Who's this? And who's running against him?'" (Goldmacher 2018). Crowley also released his own campaign video on the Internet, which received fewer than 90,000 views prior to election day. In contrast to Ocasio-Cortez's portrayal of herself as an active member of the diverse community she hoped to represent, Crowley's pitch presented him as someone with "the ability to put myself in other people's shoes" (Goldmacher 2018).

As the race showed signs of tightening, national organizers Saikat Chakrabarti, Corbin Trent, and Alexandra Rojas left other progressive campaigns sponsored by BNC and Justice Democrats to focus on NY-14. In the closing weeks, Ocasio-Cortez received endorsements from a number of liberal organizations, including MoveOn.org, the Black Lives Caucus, the Democratic Socialists of America, and People for Bernie Sanders. The only sitting member of Congress to endorse her was Representative Ro Khanna (D-CA). "This is the type of person who deserves to have a shot to serve," he stated. "She's doing it for all the right reasons" (Relman 2019). Meanwhile, Crowley received endorsements from dozens of labor unions, law enforcement organizations, and advocacy groups in the areas of gun control, women's rights, environmental protection, and LGBTQ rights. He also tallied the support of more than fifty state and federal elected officials.

On June 15, only eleven days before voters went to the polls, the two candidates made their only joint appearance of the campaign on the political talk show *Inside City Hall* on NY1 television. Rather than a formal debate, it took the form of a joint interview conducted by the program's host, journalist Errol Louis. In her opening remarks, Ocasio-Cortez emphasized the differences between herself and the incumbent, whom she portrayed as a career politician who represented the interests of his corporate donors rather than those of his constituents. "In a district that is 85 percent Democrat, overwhelmingly working class, and 70 percent people of color, we deserve a working-class champion," she said (Gray 2018). A reviewer for the left-leaning Intercept news site wrote that "Ocasio-Cortez presented as a well-studied newcomer with natural talent: delivering a summary of her agenda in a manner which was confident and sharp" (Gray 2018).

Crowley's opening remarks focused on his experience and proven leadership on the national stage, which he said put him in a strong position to resist the Trump administration's agenda. "It's not enough to fight Trump," Ocasio-Cortez responded. "We have to fight the issues that made his rise [possible] in the first place" (Gray 2018). The candidates took turns answering questions from the moderator about both local and national issues. Although they had areas of agreement, they also sparred with each other on several occasions. Ocasio-Cortez scored points during an exchange regarding a real-estate development Crowley had supported. When he claimed the development had been popular with neighborhood residents and received approval from the community board, Ocasio-Cortez corrected him by noting that she had attended the meeting in question to protest against the project, and that the board had voted overwhelmingly against it.

Although a *New York Times* editorial asserted that "both candidates held their own" in the televised debate (Editorial Board 2018), the Intercept writer asserted that Crowley often seemed flat-footed and rusty, like "a professional who felt confident enough to not prepare—and who realized too late that he should have" (Gray 2018). *Nation* analyst Raina Lipsitz commented that Ocasio-Cortez "dominated" the incumbent in their only face-to-face meeting. "She is a natural performer and a true believer, and it's thrilling to observe," she wrote. "[Ocasio-Cortez is] full of righteous fury and matching political conviction, yet clear and controlled and unafraid of the camera. . . . You can imagine her changing the world" (Lipsitz 2018).

A few days later, on June 18, the two candidates were supposed to square off again at a debate in the Bronx sponsored by the *Parkchester Times*. Citing a "scheduling conflict," Crowley declined to participate and sent a surrogate—former New York City council member Annabel Palma—to take his place. His decision prompted *The New York Times* to opine, "Mr. Crowley's constituents might well now wonder whether he intends, if re-elected, to have Ms. Palma make his floor speeches and cast his votes as well" (Editorial Board 2018). Ocasio-Cortez expressed disappointment on behalf of voters, claiming that Crowley's absence made them feel hurt and neglected. "I understand he hasn't been challenged for 14 years," she stated, "but that doesn't mean that an election isn't happening. In fact, what's happening right now is historic and it's an opportunity to show up for the community" (Krieg 2018). She also remarked on the fact that Crowley sent a Latina city official as his replacement, calling it "a bizarre twist" to end up debating "a woman with a slight resemblance to me" instead of her opponent (Lewis 2018).

Crowley's decision to skip the primary debate in favor of attending a civic association meeting in Queens generated negative publicity for his campaign. Palma often appeared unfamiliar with Crowley's policy positions, and the moderator had to remind her several times to focus on the congressman's political record rather than her own. Ocasio-Cortez took advantage of the opportunity to promote her own platform and emphasize her commitment to serving the community. A *New York Times* editorial came down hard on the incumbent, arguing that he took voters for granted and treated them like "chopped liver." "The snubs should be galling not only to Ms. Ocasio-Cortez and Mr. Crowley's constituents in New York's 14th Congressional District, in Queens and the Bronx, but also to anyone who cares about the democratic process," the editors wrote. "Mr. Crowley has decades of experience that can serve his constituents well in Congress. But his seat is not his entitlement. He'd better hope that voters don't react to his snubs by sending someone else to do the job" (Editorial Board 2018).

MACHINE POLITICS IN NEW YORK CITY

Alexandria Ocasio-Cortez once characterized her insurgent bid to unseat Representative Joseph Crowley in the 2018 Democratic primary as an effort to tear down "the last vestiges of Tammany Hall" (Pazmino 2018)—a reference to the powerful political machine that dominated New York City politics from the mid-1800s into the twentieth century. Machines were Democratic political organizations led by influential "bosses" that used a variety of methods to maintain political, legal, and administrative control over large American cities. Machine politics originated as a means to impose order and deliver services during a time of massive immigration and rapid growth. Political machines tended to have a hierarchical structure that extended from the boss—usually a city mayor or party leader, such as William M. "Boss" Tweed (1823–1873) of Tammany Hall—down to neighborhood and block organizers. Although the machines built loyal voter bases by providing jobs, housing, and other favors to poor and immigrant families, they also enriched their bosses through fraud, corruption, and political patronage.

Although reform movements largely ended the era of machine politics by the 1960s, political patronage remained an important factor in New York City politics into the twenty-first century. Incumbent politicians and party leaders often used their power and influence to ensure that their preferred candidates appeared on the ballot and received campaign financing and electoral support. "It wasn't easy to get elected in New York City without support from one of the county political machines," wrote Politico contributor Gloria Pazmino. "From the obscure City Council staffer to the state judge, county party organizations—with roots stretching back to Tammany Hall—reached into every corner of city politics and governance" (Pazmino 2018). As chair of the Queens County Democratic Party and one of the most powerful Democrats in the U.S. Congress, Crowley wielded a great deal of influence at the local, state, and federal levels. Ocasio-Cortez's primary victory over Crowley thus brought the political establishment "crashing down in spectacular fashion" (Pazmino 2018).

FURTHER READING

Budds, Diana. 2018. "The Brilliance of Alexandria Ocasio-Cortez's Bold Campaign Design." Vox, July 2, 2018. https://www.vox .com/policy-and-politics/2018/7/2/17519414/ocasio-cortez-cam paign-design-campaign-posters-tandem-branding.

Cadigan, Hilary. 2018. "Alexandria Ocasio-Cortez Learned Her Most Important Lessons from Restaurants." *Bon Appetit*, November 7, 2018. https://www.yahoo.com/lifestyle/alexandria-ocasio-cortez-learned-her-141500873.html.

Chávez, Aida, and Ryan Grim. 2018. "A Primary against the Machine: A Bronx Activist Looks to Dethrone Joseph Crowley, the King of Queens." The Intercept, May 22, 2018. https://thein tercept.com/2018/05/22/joseph-crowley-alexandra-ocasio-cortez-new-york-primary/.

Editorial Board. 2018. "If You Want to Be Speaker, Mr. Crowley, Don't Take Voters for Granted." *The New York Times*, June 19, 2018. https://www.nytimes.com/2018/06/19/opinion/joseph-crowley-alexandria-ocasio-cortez.html.

Freedlander, David. 2019a. "How Alexandria Ocasio-Cortez Broke All the Rules of New York Politics." Politico, April 8, 2019. https:// www.politico.com/magazine/story/2019/04/08/alexandria-ocasio-cortez-new-york-226578.

Freedlander, David. 2019b. "There Is Going to Be a War within the Party. We Are Going to Lean into It." Politico, February 4, 2019. https://www.politico.com/magazine/story/2019/02/04/the-insurgents-behind-alexandria-ocasio-cortez-224542.

Goldmacher, Shane. 2018. "An Upset in the Making: Why Joe Crowley Never Saw Defeat Coming." *The New York Times*, June 27, 2018. https://www.nytimes.com/2018/06/27/nyregion/ocasio-cortez-crowley-primary-upset.html.

Goldmacher, Shane, and Jonathan Martin. 2018. "Alexandria Ocasio-Cortez Defeats Joseph Crowley in Major Democratic House Upset." *The New York Times*, June 28, 2018. https://www.nytimes .com/2018/06/26/nyregion/joseph-crowley-ocasio-cortez-demo cratic-primary.html.

Gray, Briahna. 2018. "Two Very Different Democrats, Joe Crowley and Alexandria Ocasio-Cortez, Squared Off in Debate

Friday Night." The Intercept, June 16, 2018. https://theintercept
.com/2018/06/16/two-very-different-democrats-joe-crowley-and-
alexandria-ocasio-cortez-squared-off-in-debate-friday-night/.

Joyce, A. P. 2018. "Meet the Young Progressive Latina Trying to
Oust One of the Most Powerful Democrats in the House." Mic,
February 28, 2018. https://mic.com/articles/187994/meet-the-
young-progressive-latina-trying-to-oust-one-of-the-most-power
ful-democrats-in-the-house#.08z6OhhQS.

Krieg, Gregory. 2018. "A 28-Year-Old Socialist Just Ousted a Powerful, 10-Term Congressman in New York." CNN, June 27, 2018.
https://www.cnn.com/2018/06/26/politics/alexandria-ocasio-cor
tez-joe-crowley-new-york-14-primary/index.html.

Lambiet, Jose. 2019. "Exclusive: 'God Played Quite a Joke on Me with
This Politics Stuff.'" Daily Mail, March 4, 2019. https://www.dai
lymail.co.uk/news/article-6748793/Alexandria-Ocasio-Cortezs-
mother-tells-hopes-daughter-marries-longtime-boyfriend.html.

Lears, Rachel. 2019. Knock Down the House [documentary film]. Netflix. New York: Jubilee Films.

Lewis, Rebecca C. 2018. "Crowley Sends 'Worst NYC Lawmaker' to
Debate in His Place." City and State New York, June 19, 2018.
https://www.cityandstateny.com/articles/politics/news-politics/
joe-crowley-sends-annabel-palma-to-debate-in-his-place.

Lipsitz, Raina. 2018. "Alexandria Ocasio-Cortez Fights the Power."
Nation, June 22, 2018. https://www.thenation.com/article/
alexandria-ocasio-cortez-fights-power/.

Ocasio-Cortez, Alexandria. 2018. "The Courage to Change"
[video]. YouTube, May 30, 2018. https://www.youtube.com/
watch?v=rq3QXIVR0bs.

Paiella, Gabriella. 2018. "The 28-Year-Old at the Center of One of This
Year's Most Exciting Primaries." New York Magazine, June 25,
2018. https://www.thecut.com/2018/06/alexandria-ocasio-cor
tez-interview.html.

Pazmino, Gloria. 2018. "New York City Political Leaders Grapple with Life
after the Machine." Politico, June 27, 2018. https://www.politico.
com/states/new-york/albany/story/2018/06/27/new-york-city-
political-leaders-grapple-with-life-after-the-machine-492650.

Relman, Eliza. 2019. "The Truth about Alexandria Ocasio-Cortez." *Insider*, January 6, 2019. https://www.thisisinsider.com/alexandria-ocasio-cortez-biography-2019-1.

Remnick, David. 2018. "Alexandria Ocasio-Cortez's Historic Win and the Future of the Democratic Party." *The New Yorker*, July 16, 2018. https://www.newyorker.com/magazine/2018/07/23/alexandria-ocasio-cortezs-historic-win-and-the-future-of-the-democratic-party.

Steiger, Kay. 2018. "Is a High-Ranking House Democrat about to Lose His Primary?" Vox, June 26, 2018. https://www.vox.com/policy-and-politics/2018/6/26/17501194/crowley-ocasio-cortez-new-york-primary-midterms-democrats.

Stuart, Tessa. 2018. "Alexandria Ocasio-Cortez: 'I Lean into the Misconceptions.'" *Rolling Stone*, October 8, 2018. https://www.rollingstone.com/politics/politics-features/alexandria-ocasio-cortez-interview-2-732173/.

Chapter 6

VICTORY FOR THE
UNDERDOG

Nobody's ever supposed to win their first bid for office. Nobody's ever supposed to win without taking lobbyists' money, no one's ever supposed to defeat an incumbent, no one's ever supposed to run a grassroots campaign without running any ads on television. We did all of those things. (Feller 2018)

On June 26, 2018, voters in New York City went to the polls for the primary elections. Candidates who prevailed in the primary races earned the right to represent their political parties on the ballot for the general election. The race between Alexandria Ocasio-Cortez and Representative Joseph Crowley in the Fourteenth Congressional District carried even higher stakes. Since registered Democrats outnumbered registered Republicans by a 6–1 margin in NY-14, the winner of the Democratic primary would be virtually guaranteed to prevail in the November general election and secure a seat in the 116th U.S. Congress.

Staff members, volunteers, and supporters of Ocasio-Cortez's campaign gathered at a billiards hall in the Bronx to watch the election returns. When Ocasio-Cortez and her partner, Riley Roberts, arrived at the event, they notice a group of reporters running down the street toward them. Ocasio-Cortez rushed inside and saw the final vote tallies scroll across a television monitor. "I hadn't checked any of the polls on my phone," she recalled. "I'm literally racing these reporters into the billiards hall, and I run . . . to this TV set and I look up and I see the margin, and then I see the amount of precincts reporting. And that's how I found out that we won the election. Right there in that moment" (Park 2018).

Ocasio-Cortez received 15,897 votes, compared to 11,761 for her opponent. She defeated the powerful ten-term incumbent congressman by 15 percentage points, 57 percent to 42 percent. A film crew captured her startled reaction at the moment she first realized that she had won. The viral video shows a wide-eyed Ocasio-Cortez clasp her hands over her mouth in disbelief, repeat "Oh my God" several times, and then thank her excited supporters. "We meet a machine with a movement, and that is what we have done today," she declared in her victory speech. "Working-class Americans want a clear champion, and there is nothing radical about moral clarity in 2018" (Park 2018).

Political observers across the country were equally surprised to learn of Ocasio-Cortez's primary victory. The *Guardian* described it as "a stunning political upset that sent shockwaves through the party" (Jacobs and Gambino 2018), while *The New York Times* called it "the most significant loss for a Democratic incumbent in more than a decade" (Goldmacher and Martin 2018). Many media outlets compared Ocasio-Cortez's unexpected triumph to the 2014 Republican primary for Virginia's Seventh Congressional District, in which an unknown Tea Party candidate, economics professor Dave Brat, unseated House Majority Leader Eric Cantor.

At a gathering of his supporters in Queens, Crowley conceded the race and promised to back his opponent in the general election and beyond. "I want to congratulate Ms. Ocasio-Cortez on her victory tonight," he said. "I look forward to supporting her and all Democrats this November. The Trump administration is a threat to everything we stand for here in Queens and the Bronx, and if we don't win back the House this November, we will lose the nation we love" (Krieg 2018). Crowley then picked up a guitar and dedicated a song to Ocasio-Cortez, Bruce Springsteen's 1975 classic "Born to Run."

Ocasio-Cortez received congratulatory messages from dozens of prominent Democrats, including Hillary Clinton and Nancy Pelosi. Senator Bernie Sanders also praised the performance of his former campaign organizer. "She took on the entire local Democratic establishment in her district and won a very strong victory," he said. "She demonstrated once again what progressive grassroots politics can do" (Resnick 2018). President Donald Trump commented on the race on Twitter, expressing satisfaction that one of his political opponents would be leaving Congress. "Wow! Big Trump Hater Congressman Joe Crowley, who many expected was going to take Nancy Pelosi's place, just LOST his primary election," he wrote. "In other words, he's out! That is a big one that nobody saw happening. Perhaps he should have been nicer, and more respectful, to his President!" (Resnick 2018).

ANALYZING HER VICTORY

Political commentators immediately began dissecting the race and speculating about the factors that had contributed to Ocasio-Cortez's victory. Some claimed that the changing demographics of the district played a major role in generating support for the challenger and limiting support for the incumbent. Redistricting in 2012 had changed the boundaries of NY-14, removing the historic Maspeth neighborhood and other parts of Queens that had traditionally been regarded as Crowley strongholds. The redrawn district was more diverse and more liberal than before. "A lot of people of color were excited about a young woman of color," said Michael Blake, a New York assemblyman and Democratic National Committee vice chairman. "People say demographics are destiny and you can't ignore that reality when looking at the numbers there" (Goldmacher 2018).

Ocasio-Cortez rejected the assertion that she won the election because of her ethnicity. "It would be a huge mistake to just say that this election happened because X demographics live here," she stated. "That is to absolutely miss the entire point of what we just accomplished" (Goldmacher 2018). An analysis of the election results supported her position, showing that she captured Crowley's home borough of Queens by a larger margin than her own home borough of the Bronx. Ocasio-Cortez contended that the ideas she promoted in her campaign—such as Medicare for All and a federal jobs guarantee—held broad appeal for voters in her district. "I think a lot of working-class Americans and voters here have been waiting for an unapologetic champion for economic, social, and racial dignity in the United States," she said. "And we provided a very direct message, a very clear message" (Jacobs and Gambino 2018).

Some analysts viewed Ocasio-Cortez's success against an established incumbent as evidence of a progressive shift among Democratic voters that began with Sanders's 2016 campaign. Convinced that the status quo was no longer working, many Democrats called for bold policies and fresh leadership to better position the party to face future challenges. "Many voters, particularly young people, understand the time for incrementalism and moderation is long over," contended journalist Ross Barkan in the *Guardian*. "Democrats like Ocasio-Cortez comprehend this. They aren't going to Washington to compromise, to shake hands with an enemy that would prefer to kick the working class, the poor, and people of color to the gutter and leave them there" (Barkan 2018).

Other commentators noted that Democratic women became more politically active and energized following Trump's election, resulting in historic numbers of female candidates seeking and winning office. Liberal women defeated more moderate men in several other Democratic primaries in 2018. The list of winners included Kara Eastman in Nebraska, Amy McGrath in Kentucky, Katie Porter in California, and Kathleen Williams in Montana. Yet Representative Nancy Pelosi, the top-ranking Democrat in the House, warned against interpreting Ocasio-Cortez's victory as part of a larger trend. "They made a choice in one district," she stated. "The fact that in a very progressive district in New York, it went more progressive . . . is about that district. It is not to be viewed as something that stands for anything else" (Jacobs and Gambino 2018).

Some political insiders blamed Crowley for his defeat, arguing that he ran an old-fashioned and uninspired campaign. "We had people running this like a 1998 City Council race and not a 2018 congressional primary," said one campaign worker (Goldmacher 2018). Although Crowley outspent Ocasio-Cortez by a 10–1 margin, the approach taken by his Queens Democratic machine often seemed antiquated in comparison to the one used by her army of progressive activists. "She ran a very effective campaign. And I ran a very traditional campaign, an incumbent campaign," Crowley acknowledged. "And I would say this, the loss is on me. I accept this. You know, the shortcomings, we had a strategy that didn't work. And hers did. And I congratulate her for that" (Villa 2018).

Crowley's campaign strategy targeted people identified as likely voters, most of whom had turned out for primary elections before. In contrast, Ocasio-Cortez's campaign strategy focused on energizing the people most likely to support her progressive platform—including young people, immigrants, and working-class families—and getting them to the polls. Nick Haby, a resident of the middle-class Astoria neighborhood of Queens who switched his allegiance from Crowley to Ocasio-Cortez midway through the primary race, recalled that "almost every person I talked to while canvassing for Alex had an excitement and enthusiasm for her that I did not see in the people supporting Joe Crowley" (Marans 2018).

Ocasio-Cortez's campaign team identified 76,000 individuals who met their criteria and made contact with each person three ways: in person, by telephone, and via e-mail. They also made extensive use of social media to promote the candidate's ideas and events. Ocasio-Cortez claimed that her successful campaign proved the effectiveness of progressive organizing tactics. "You have given this country proof that when you knock on your neighbor's door, when you come to them with love, when you let them know that no matter your stance, you are there for them—that we can make change," she said (Krieg 2018).

Some observers attributed the surprising election results to a combination of all of these factors. "If it takes a perfect storm to dislodge a congressional leader, then Ms. Ocasio-Cortez and her crusading campaign about class, race, gender, age, absenteeism, and ideology proved to be just that," Shane Goldmacher wrote in *The New York Times*. "No single factor led to Mr. Crowley's defeat. . . . It was demographics and generational change, insider versus outsider, traditional tactics versus modern-age digital organizing. It was the cumulative weight of them all" (Goldmacher 2018).

LEVERAGING HER FAME

Ocasio-Cortez's unexpected primary victory generated national media attention and made her an instant political star. Few traditional media outlets had provided much coverage of her campaign before she won. In fact, Ocasio-Cortez once noted on Twitter that the headlines in New York newspapers always referred to her as Crowley's opponent rather than mentioning her by name. Aside from a *Vogue* interview that appeared the day before the primary, profiles of the underdog candidate only appeared in online media outlets dedicated to progressive politics, such as The Young Turks and The Intercept. "The traditional media pay attention to one metric—money—but there should be other considerations: number of volunteers, social-media engagement, small-dollar donations," said Cenk Uygur of The Young Turks. "And she was through the roof on all of those metrics" (Sullivan 2018). In the days following the election, however, Ocasio-Cortez received interview requests from hundreds of media outlets, including newspapers, magazines, radio stations, television news programs, and late-night talk shows.

After spending a year campaigning in relative obscurity, Ocasio-Cortez found some aspects of her sudden fame surreal. When dozens of admirers asked about the lipstick she wore during election-night interviews, for instance, Ocasio-Cortez obliged by revealing the name on Twitter: Stila Stay All Day® Liquid in Beso. The following day, the brand sold out online, which prevented even Ocasio-Cortez from obtaining more. In another indication of national interest, the Merriam-Webster online dictionary site's Trend Watch noted that searches for the word "socialism" increased by 1,500 percent on June 27, the day after Ocasio-Cortez's primary win. When she appeared as a guest on *The Late Show with Stephen Colbert*, the host admitted that one day earlier he had never heard of her. Within a matter of days, however, Ocasio-Cortez gained so much name recognition that people all across the country began referring to her by her initials: AOC.

Not all of the attention Ocasio-Cortez received was positive. She became a target of scorn and derision among many conservative and right-wing commentators, who found her youth, political inexperience, outspokenness, and socialist ideas alarming. "You can hardly go

anywhere in conservative media—Fox, talk radio, conservative magazines and websites, Twitter and other social media—without seeing
somebody mocking or criticizing her," Dan McLaughlin wrote in the
National Review. "Some conservatives wisely fret that our side is just
helping create a monster by elevating the profile of a glib young person
on the other side with star power" (McLaughlin 2019).

Among progressives, however, Ocasio-Cortez became one of the
most in-demand figures at fundraising events and on the campaign
trail. She was the "undisputed star" of the 2018 Netroots Nation, an
annual conference for progressive organizers and activists that also featured keynote addresses by several Democratic senators with presidential aspirations, including Elizabeth Warren, Kamala Harris, and Cory
Booker. In her speech, Ocasio-Cortez urged Democrats to return to the
progressive foundations that Franklin D. Roosevelt built with his New
Deal social welfare programs. "It's time to remember that universal college education, trade school, a federal jobs guarantee, exploration of a
universal basic income were not proposed in 2016, they were proposed
in 1940 by a Democratic President of the United States," she declared.
"These are not new ideas. We are picking up where we last left off,
when we were last most powerful" (Alter 2018).

Ocasio-Cortez leveraged her fame and political capital to endorse several other progressive candidates who were running for Congress with
the support of Justice Democrats and Brand New Congress, including
Ayanna Pressley in Massachusetts and Cori Bush in Missouri. Ocasio-
Cortez explained that she wanted to help elect a caucus of Democratic
legislators who were free from corporate influence and committed to
advancing progressive goals. Her endorsements generated awareness,
donations, and volunteers for the selected campaigns. Pressley gained
5,000 Twitter followers within 24 hours after Ocasio-Cortez urged her
own followers to "vote her in next" (DeCosta-Klipa 2018). Bush, who
decided to challenge a longtime Democratic incumbent after organizing Black Lives Matter protests on the streets of Ferguson, said that
Ocasio-Cortez's endorsement "totally changed our race. . . . All my
social media went nuts, my email went nuts, and donations took off
exponentially" (Wang 2018).

Ocasio-Cortez's primary victory brought energy and legitimacy to
other women's candidacy by proving that a strong campaign could

overcome long odds. "What I've seen is a lot of activity on Twitter and Facebook of women saying, 'Hey, pay attention to these other women,'" Bush said. "We were doing it before, but after Tuesday, now it's like, 'Hey, no, pay attention, because this is for real. These women can win if we just get behind them'" (Wang 2018). The record number of women running for office in 2018 launched a trend toward greater political collaboration, as female candidates forged alliances, devised strategies, offered advice, shared resources, and amplified each other's campaigns and platforms. "They're folks that aren't necessarily endorsed by the party or don't have access to the party networks," political science professor Kelly Dittmar explained. "So in order to build that support base—among voters, but especially in terms of finances and volunteers—they have to build something new or at least draw from existing infrastructure for progressive candidates" (Wang 2018).

FOCUSING ON THE GENERAL ELECTION

In the fall of 2018, Ocasio-Cortez shifted her focus back toward her own congressional campaign. Even though her district leaned heavily Democratic, she still faced opposition in her bid for a seat in the U.S. House of Representatives. The Republican Party nominated Anthony Pappas, a 72-year-old Astoria resident who taught economics and finance at St. John's University, but did not provide any financial or logistical support to his campaign. Surprisingly, Joseph Crowley also appeared on the ballot as the candidate of the Working Families Party (WFP). At one point, Ocasio-Cortez grew concerned that Crowley planned to mount a third-party challenge to retain his seat. She posted a message on Twitter reminding voters—as well as the incumbent—that he had already conceded defeat in the primary and promised to endorse her. Crowley responded by tweeting, "Alexandria, the race is over and Democrats need to come together. I've made my support for you clear and the fact that I'm not running" (Lovett 2018). He also claimed that New York election laws made it impossible for him to remove his name from the ballot.

Despite Crowley's assurances, the controversy surrounding his candidacy resurfaced in July, when former senator Joseph Lieberman of Connecticut publicly encouraged Crowley to resume his campaign.

Lieberman, who successfully ran for office as an independent after losing a Democratic primary in 2006, argued in a *Wall Street Journal* editorial that Ocasio-Cortez would not be an effective legislator because her ideas were too far left of the mainstream Democratic Party. In response, the WFP formally endorsed Ocasio-Cortez and withdrew its support for Crowley, urging its members not to vote for the incumbent. "WFP is giving all we have to electing Ocasio-Cortez and other progressive insurgents all across the nation," said New York WFP director Bill Lipton (Lovett 2018). Ocasio-Cortez also received endorsements from many high-profile Democrats, including Sanders and former president Barack Obama.

Ocasio-Cortez experienced a poignant moment at the end of her general election campaign, when actress Kate Mulgrew attended one of her campaign rallies in New York City. Mulgrew was best known for her role as Captain Kathryn Janeway on the television series *Star Trek: Voyager* (1995–2001). As the first female starship captain in the *Star Trek* franchise, Janeway inspired Ocasio-Cortez and many other young women with her strong leadership and dedication to science and technology. Ocasio-Cortez grew up watching episodes of *Voyager* with her father, and they shared that experience one last time in his hospital room shortly before he died. "In one scene, Captain Janeway appears and my husband, who could no longer talk, pointed at the captain then at Alexandria, and back and forth, to say to her he thought she'd be like Captain Janeway one day, someone in charge," her mother, Blanca, remembered. "We didn't think anything of it. Then, who showed up on the stage of Alexandria's last rally before the general election in the Bronx 10 years later? . . . My daughter was speechless. For once" (Lambiet 2019). Mulgrew was delighted to learn of the candidate's connection to her character and presented Ocasio-Cortez with an honorary Star Trek badge.

When voters went to the polls on November 6, they resolved any lingering questions surrounding the election by overwhelmingly choosing Ocasio-Cortez. She received 110,318 votes, or 78 percent of those cast, compared to 19,202 for Pappas (14 percent) and 9,348 for Crowley (7 percent). Having celebrated her 29th birthday three weeks earlier, Ocasio-Cortez thus became the youngest woman ever elected to the U.S. Congress. "We made history tonight," she declared in a victory speech to a crowd of supporters. "This is what is possible when everyday people come together in the collective realization that all our actions, no matter how small or how large, are powerful, worthwhile and capable of lasting change. . . . There is never any fight that is too big for us to pick. We proved that this year. Because in the wealthiest nation in the history of the world, our greatest scarcity is not a lack of resources but the absence of political courage and moral imagination" (Herrerla 2018).

NETROOTS NATION

In August 2018, only five weeks after her unexpected primary win, Alexandria Ocasio-Cortez gave a keynote address on the final day of the Netroots Nation convention in New Orleans, Louisiana. Netroots Nation is a gathering of progressive political leaders, campaign workers, organizers, and activists that has been held annually since 2007, when Democratic presidential candidate Barack Obama addressed attendees. Each three-day event features training sessions for activists, panel discussions on current issues, keynote addresses by political figures, and opportunities for progressives to exchange ideas and build a sense of community. Bloggers and readers of the liberal news site Daily Kos originally coined the term "Netroots" by combining the words "Internet" and "grassroots."

The Netroots Nation conference has historically served as a forum for progressive activists to establish priorities and set an agenda for the left wing of the Democratic Party, which has sometimes led to infighting between different factions and interests. The 2018 conference featured "a tug-of-war between its old guard and its newcomers" (Alter 2018). Old-guard Democrats pushed a centrist platform intended to regain the support of white moderate "swing voters" who voted for Donald Trump in 2016. New-generation Democrats, who became politically active in response to Trump's election, argued that the party should promote progressive policies to attract millennials, women, and people of color.

For many attendees, Ocasio-Cortez represented the new face of the Democratic Party. "By virtue of her identity, her message, and her online medium," said journalist Eliza Relman, "Ocasio-Cortez is speaking directly to young people, immigrants, and people of color, the nontraditional voters Democrats must energize" (Relman 2019). Ocasio-Cortez asserted that inspiring candidates and grassroots organizing, rather than centrist policies, would attract voters to the Democratic Party. "People think swing voters are political moderates. They're not," she stated. "It's not that the candidate has to accommodate the swing voter. It's that if the candidate is compelling enough, the voter will swing to that candidate's politics" (Aleksander 2018).

FURTHER READING

Aleksander, Irina. 2018. "How Alexandria Ocasio-Cortez and Other Progressives Are Defining the Midterms." *Vogue*, October 15, 2018. https://www.vogue.com/article/alexandria-ocasio-cortez-interview-vogue-november-2018-issue.

Alter, Charlotte. 2018. "The Democratic Divide Isn't between Left and Center. It's between Old and New." *Time*, August 6, 2018. http://time.com/5359100/democrats-netroots/.

Barkan, Ross. 2018. "Alexandria Ocasio-Cortez Represents the Future of the Democratic Party." *Guardian*, June 27, 2018. https://www.theguardian.com/commentisfree/2018/jun/27/alexandria-ocasio-cortez-future-democratic-party.

DeCosta-Klipa, Nik. 2018. "'Vote Her in Next': Alexandria Ocasio-Cortez Calls on Massachusetts for Next Political Upset." *Boston Globe*, June 27, 2018. https://www.boston.com/news/politics/2018/06/27/alexandria-ocasio-cortez-ayanna-pressley.

Feller, Madison. 2018. "Alexandria Ocasio-Cortez Knows She Can't Save America All by Herself." *Elle*, July 16, 2018. https://www.elle.com/culture/career-politics/a22118408/alexandria-ocasio-cortez-interview/.

Goldmacher, Shane. 2018. "An Upset in the Making: Why Joe Crowley Never Saw Defeat Coming." *The New York Times*, June 27, 2018. https://www.nytimes.com/2018/06/27/nyregion/ocasio-cortez-crowley-primary-upset.html.

Goldmacher, Shane, and Jonathan Martin. 2018. "Alexandria Ocasio-Cortez Defeats Joseph Crowley in Major Democratic House Upset." *The New York Times*, June 28, 2018. https://www.nytimes.com/2018/06/26/nyregion/joseph-crowley-ocasio-cortez-democratic-primary.html.

Herrerla, Carla. 2018. "Ocasio-Cortez Proclaims 'We Made History' in Electrifying Victory Speech." *Huffington Post*, November 7, 2018. https://www.huffpost.com/entry/alexandria-ocasio-cortez-victory-speech-midterms_n_5be26e7ee4b0dbe871a46631.

Jacobs, Ben, and Lauren Gambino. 2018. "Democrats See Major Upset as Socialist Beats Top-Ranking U.S. Congressman." *Guardian*, June 27, 2018. https://www.theguardian.com/us-news/2018/jun/26/democrats-primaries-upset-joe-crowley-alexandria-osacio-cortez.

Krieg, Gregory. 2018. "A 28-Year-Old Socialist Just Ousted a Powerful, 10-Term Congressman in New York." CNN, June 27, 2018. https://www.cnn.com/2018/06/26/politics/alexandria-ocasio-cortez-joe-crowley-new-york-14-primary/index.html.

Lambiet, Jose. 2019. "Exclusive: 'God Played Quite a Joke on Me with This Politics Stuff.'" *Daily Mail*, March 4, 2019. https://www.dailymail.co.uk/news/article-6748793/Alexandria-Ocasio-Cortezs-mother-tells-hopes-daughter-marries-longtime-boyfriend.html.

Lovett, Kenneth. 2018. "Ocasio-Cortez Rips Crowley for Not Giving Up Working Families Party Line." *New York Daily News*, July 12, 2018. https://www.nydailynews.com/news/politics/ny-pol-ocasio-cortez-crowley-working-families-party-20180712-story.html.

Marans, Daniel. 2018. "How Alexandria Ocasio-Cortez Caught Fire and Took Down the King of Queens." *Huffington Post*, June 28, 2018. https://www.huffpost.com/entry/how-alexandria-ocasio-cortez-caught-fire-took-down-joe-crowley_n_5b34ec7ce4b0b5e692f57206.

McLaughlin, Dan. 2019. "Why Does Alexandria Ocasio-Cortez Get So Much Attention from the Right?" *National Review*, January 4, 2019. https://www.nationalreview.com/corner/why-does-alexandria-ocasio-cortez-get-so-much-attention-from-the-right/.

Park, Andrea. 2018. "Alexandria Ocasio-Cortez Explains Democratic Socialism on the 'Late Show.'" CBS News, June 29, 2018. https://www.cbsnews.com/news/alexandria-ocasio-cortez-explains-democratic-socialism-on-the-late-show/.

Relman, Eliza. 2019. "The Truth about Alexandria Ocasio-Cortez." Insider, January 6, 2019. https://www.thisisinsider.com/alexandria-ocasio-cortez-biography-2019-1.

Resnick, Gideon. 2018. "Young Progressive Alexandria Ocasio-Cortez Topples Old Boss Joe Crowley in Democratic Primary Shocker." Daily Beast, June 26, 2018. https://www.thedailybeast.com/young-progressive-alexandria-ocasio-cortez-topples-old-boss-joe-crowley-in-democratic-primary-shocker.

Sullivan, Margaret. 2018. "Alexandria Ocasio-Cortez's Victory Points to a Media Failure That Keeps Repeating." *The Washington Post*, June 28, 2018. https://www.washingtonpost.com/lifestyle/style/alexandria-ocasio-cortezs-victory-points-to-a-media-failure-that-keeps-repeating/2018/06/28/68f05130–7aca-11e8–93cc-6d3beccdd7a3_story.html?utm_term=.4e9919aeae9e.

Villa, Lissandra. 2018. "Joe Crowley Says Millennials Kicked Him Out of Congress." BuzzFeed News, October 7, 2018. https://www.buzzfeednews.com/article/lissandravilla/joe-crowley-alexandria-ocasio-cortez-millennials-democrats?bfsource=relatedmanual.

Wang, Vivian. 2018. "Ocasio-Cortez's Next Task: Empowering Other Female Outsiders to Win." *The New York Times*, July 6, 2018. https://www.nytimes.com/2018/07/06/nyregion/ocasio-cortez-effect-election-democrat.html.

Chapter 7

MEMBER OF CONGRESS

We need to realize that our democracy does belong to us, and that if we don't participate in it, we don't invest in it, we don't put our own energy into it, what we're doing is we're giving it away to somebody else. We give it away to a very small group of people. (Castillo 2019)

When Alexandria Ocasio-Cortez became the youngest woman ever elected to the U.S. House of Representatives, she joined a group of legislators that *The New York Times* called "the most racially diverse and most female group of representatives ever elected to the House, whose history spans more than 200 years" (Edmondson and Lee 2019). Following the 2018 midterm elections, the House featured a record total of 102 women, up from 84 in the previous session, leading some commentators to refer to it as "the year of the woman."

The total also included a record forty women of color, including several besides Ocasio-Cortez who broke barriers with their victories. Ilhan Omar (D-MN) and Rashida Tlaib (D-MI) became the first Muslim women elected to Congress, for instance, while Sharice Davids (D-KS) and Deb Haaland (D-NM) became the first Native American women elected to Congress. Ayanna Pressley (D-MA), who joined Ocasio-Cortez in unseating a long-serving Democratic incumbent in the primary, became the first black woman elected to Congress from Massachusetts, while Jahana Hayes (D-CT) earned the same distinction in Connecticut. Sylvia Garcia (D-TX) and Veronica Escobar (D-TX) became the first Latinas elected from Texas.

Ocasio-Cortez was one of 37 women—all but 2 of them Democrats—to become first-time House members. The freshman class of the 116th Congress also included 10 Hispanic members, which brought the total number of Latinos in the House to a record high of 37. Nine newly elected House members were African American, meaning that the number of black representatives also reached a new high of 55. All nine of the black first-time office holders were Democrats, and they all prevailed in predominantly white, suburban districts.

Some analysts attributed the historic diversity of the new Congress to record-setting numbers of women and minorities running for office. A total of 237 women—185 Democrats and 52 Republicans—ran for House seats in 2018. About one-third of the female candidates were women of color, which represented a 75 percent increase over 2012 (Gaudiano 2018). Many of these women attributed their political awakening to the Women's March, the #MeToo movement against sexual harassment and assault, the Never Again student movement against gun violence, and other social activism that arose as part of the anti-Trump resistance following the 2016 presidential election. "That would not be occurring without Donald Trump in the White House," said David Wasserman, an editor of the nonpartisan Cook Political Report. "It is a direct reaction to his election" (Gaudiano 2018). Of the forty House seats that flipped from Republican to Democratic hands in 2018—giving Democrats control of the chamber—60 percent were won by female candidates (Edmondson and Lee 2019).

The election results reflected a shift in public attitudes about political representation. A CNN exit poll found that 80 percent of 2018 midterm voters felt it was important for women and minorities to become more involved in American politics. Debbie Walsh, director of the Center for American Women and Politics at Rutgers University, noted that women and minorities "bring different voices, different perspectives, different life experiences . . . to the making of public policy."

She asserted that the historic diversity in the 116th Congress would open "a world of possibilities to women and people of color who will follow in their footsteps" (Madhani and Berry 2018).

PROTESTING CORPORATE INFLUENCE AT ORIENTATION

Prior to taking office, Ocasio-Cortez and other newly elected members of Congress traveled to Boston, Massachusetts, to attend a three-day orientation session at the Institute of Politics in Harvard University's Kennedy School of Government. Sponsors described the program, which incoming lawmakers have attended every election year since 1972, as "the preeminent educational and preparatory program for newly elected Republican and Democratic Members of the House of Representatives" (Newell 2018). It provided issue briefings, policy discussions, and logistical information to help freshmen legislators "forge bipartisan relationships and learn practical skills of lawmaking just one month prior to taking the oath of office" (Relman 2018a).

Although promoters described the program as bipartisan and ideologically neutral, Ocasio-Cortez disagreed with this characterization and expressed her opinion on social media. She criticized the extent of corporate influence—noting that the hosts of the event included the American Enterprise Institute, a conservative think tank funded by the billionaire brothers Charles and David Koch—and the lack of progressive input. "Our 'bipartisan' congressional orientation is co-hosted by a corporate lobbyist group," Ocasio-Cortez tweeted. "Other members have quietly expressed to me their concern that this wasn't told to us in advance. Lobbyists are here. [Wall Street investment bank] Goldman Sachs is here. Where's labor? Activists? Frontline community leaders?" (Johnson 2018).

According to promoters, the slate of speakers and panelists included "former elected office holders, current and former senior White House and administration officials, diplomats, economists, business leaders, lobbyists, and academics," who would provide the new legislators with "insights on governing" (Johnson 2018). Although twenty-five of the new House members had run and won as progressives, none of the presentations offered a progressive perspective on poverty, workers' rights, health care, immigration, environmental protection, or other issues. Until Ocasio-Cortez and Tlaib registered their protests on social media, however, most people seemed unconcerned about this dynamic. "One of the best parts of Ocasio-Cortez's arrival in DC as a new leader is that she notices, and is revolted by, the corrupt, corporatist rituals that are so embedded in DC culture that most politicians and journalists barely notice them, let alone find them objectionable or odd," wrote Glenn Greenwald on the progressive news site The Intercept (Johnson 2018).

Secretary of Transportation Elaine Chao—a member of Trump's cabinet and the wife of Senate Majority Leader Mitch McConnell, a key Trump ally in Congress—gave the opening remarks at the orientation. Ocasio-Cortez and several other newly elected progressives, including Tlaib, Pressley, and Omar, skipped the session to attend a rally. "Opening remarks is from Trump admin, so we're holding a presser on health-care and gun violence instead," Ocasio-Cortez explained on Instagram (Relman 2018a). The organizations represented at the rally included Partners in Health, a Boston-based nonprofit dedicated to providing quality health services to poor nations and communities. "Make no mistake: This new-member orientation is an orientation of the status quo," said Joia Mukherjee, its chief medical officer. "And what we are voting for is justice" (Relman 2018a).

In the wake of the protests by progressive legislators and groups, Harvard officials promised to take the criticism into consideration when putting together future programs for members of Congress. "This is a university," said Mark Gearan, director of the Institute of Politics at the Kennedy School. "Any good university reviews its curriculum, reviews its coursework, and thinks of ways we might want to go forward" (Newell 2018).

CHOOSING STAFF AND ESTABLISHING EMPLOYMENT POLICIES

As Ocasio-Cortez prepared to take her seat in Congress, she selected staff members to help run her legislative office. As her chief of staff, she appointed Saikat Chakrabarti, a former Silicon Valley technology entrepreneur who first became involved in progressive politics as an organizer for Bernie Sanders's presidential campaign. Chakrabarti cofounded Brand New Congress and Justice Democrats, the progressive groups that recruited Ocasio-Cortez to run for office, and created software applications to facilitate grassroots volunteer organizing for progressive candidates. Ocasio-Cortez chose another veteran activist from the Sanders campaign and Justice Democrats, Corbin Trent, as her communications director. Trent ran a food-truck business in Knoxville, Tennessee, before getting involved in progressive politics.

To fill out her staff, Ocasio-Cortez decided to cast a wide net in hopes of attracting progressive activists who did not fit the typical profile of the Capitol Hill establishment. Ocasio-Cortez's legislative assistant, Dan Riffle, described most congressional staffers as "careerists." "These are people who grew up on the Upper West Side and went to Ivy League schools. These are people who don't think big and aren't here to change the world," he asserted. "They only conceive of the world as it is, and work within that frame" (Stein 2019). Ocasio-Cortez received a record 5,500 applications from people who shared her priorities and wanted to help promote change. "People in this office are really . . . normal people," said Riffle, who was raised in poverty by a single mother and became a political activist in the campaign to legalize marijuana. "And in part because of that, there's a willingness to think outside the box and make mistakes—there's no other office that has that. They didn't come up in this system. So they don't know how it works. And as a result, they don't feel constrained by it" (Stein 2019).

Ocasio-Cortez made headlines by announcing that she planned to pay every member of her staff a "living wage" that would enable them to afford basic expenses in Washington, D.C., where the cost of living ranked among the highest of any American city. She devised the plan after learning that many congressional staff members and interns earned so little that they had to take second and third jobs to make ends meet. "This week I went to dive spot in DC for some late night food. I chatted up the staff. SEVERAL bartenders, managers, & servers *currently worked in Senate + House offices*," she posted on Twitter. "This is a disgrace" (Relman 2018b). Ocasio-Cortez pointed out that annual salaries for members of Congress ranged from $174,000 to $223,500, or between three and four times the median American household income of $59,000. "It is unjust for Congress to budget a living wage for ourselves, yet rely on unpaid interns and underpaid, overworked staff," she tweeted (Relman 2018b).

Ocasio-Cortez noted that her own experiences in the food-service industry helped her understand the struggles of working-class people trying to make ends meet. After the November election, she told an interviewer that she would have trouble affording an apartment in D.C. until she began collecting her government salary in January. When Fox News pundits criticized her financial situation, Ocasio-Cortez used it as an opportunity to express her views on economic inequality. "There is no reason to be ashamed or embarrassed," she wrote on Twitter. "Mocking lower incomes is exactly how those who benefit from + promote wealth inequality the most keep everyday people silent about one of the worst threats to American society: that the rich are getting richer and the poor, poorer" (Clark 2018). Ocasio-Cortez claimed that her perspective differed from that of most members of Congress since 40 percent of all federal legislators were millionaires. "Many members of Congress were born into wealth, or they grew up around it," she stated. "How can you legislate a better life for working people if you've never been a working person?" (Cadigan 2018).

In most cases, members of Congress receive a stipend of approximately $1 million per year to divide among up to eighteen paid staff members. Many legislators use a hierarchical pay system with base salaries ranging from around $28,000 per year for low-level staffers to $150,000 per year for chiefs of staff. Ocasio-Cortez upended this system and flattened the hierarchy in her office. She announced that every staff member would earn a minimum of $52,000 per year, which would enable them to afford the average $2,500 monthly rent in D.C. In order to fit all staff members within her office budget, Ocasio-Cortez also announced that she would cap staff salaries at a maximum of $80,000 per year. In addition, she planned to pay interns $15 per hour plus benefits. She offered a benefit package that included twelve weeks of paid parental leave for any staff member—male or female—who welcomed a new child into their family.

Fellow progressives praised Ocasio-Cortez for designing a workplace that reflected her commitment to expanding workers' rights, providing a living wage, and reducing income inequality. They predicted that her high entry-level salary and generous benefits package would help

her attract talented people and increase her staff's loyalty and engagement. Critics, on the other hand, suggested that the cap on upper-
level salaries might prevent Ocasio-Cortez from retaining experienced
staff members who would be tempted to take their skills to more lucra-
tive jobs in the private sector. In any case, the freshman legislator's
employment policies appeared to influence other members of Congress.
After initially posting an opening for an unpaid intern position, Senate
Minority Leader Chuck Schumer (D-NY) quickly backtracked, saying
that his office planned to pay interns and that the earlier job posting
had been made "in error" (Relman 2018b).

Ocasio-Cortez and her staff were assigned an office in the House Office
Building that had previously been occupied by Representative Barbara
Comstock (R-VA), who was unseated by a Democratic challenger in the
2018 midterm elections. Although the inside of the office had a spar-
tan, unfinished look, the wall outside the door quickly became covered
with hundreds of brightly colored sticky notes. "Some mothers came by
and left 2–3 encouraging notes on my plaque," Ocasio-Cortez recalled.
"We left them up, because it was great to read those little encouraging
words every morning. Soon, more Post-its® came. It became a little rit-
ual for the public, so we left stacks out for people" (Buncombe 2019).
Visitors posted words of support, gratitude, and praise, as well as funny
drawings, inspiring quotes, random slogans, and occasional tips, advice,
or criticism. Some observers viewed the splash of neon-colored papers
in the stark white-marble hallway as a symbol of the new energy and
ideas Ocasio-Cortez brought to Capitol Hill. Eventually, though, House
officials asked her staff to remove the notes, claiming that they violated
building rules by obstructing the Braille letters on her office nameplate.
Ocasio-Cortez kept all of the notes and displayed them on a wall inside
the office. In addition to positive messages on Post-It® notes, however,
Ocasio-Cortez also received hate mail and death threats as she prepared
to take office. The Capitol Police responded by training her staff to perform risk assessments of visitors.

SWEARING-IN CEREMONY

Throughout the transition period between her election and swearing-
in ceremony, Ocasio-Cortez documented both the exciting and the

challenging aspects of her experiences as a new legislator on social media. While touring the Library of Congress, for instance, she posted photos of its stately columns, soaring ceilings, colorful murals, and ornate sculptures with a caption referencing the Harry Potter series, "Welcome to Hogwarts." Ocasio-Cortez also shared photos of the "swag bag" given to incoming members of Congress, which contained a government-issued, high-security phone and tablet as well as a member directory or "freshman yearbook." She expressed delight upon learning about the network of tunnels beneath the Capitol building, and she expressed frustration at being mistaken for an intern or spouse rather than recognized as a legislator (Wanshel 2018). Many people who read Ocasio-Cortez's tweets or followed her stories on Instagram found her experiences relatable and praised her for making behind-the-scenes aspects of governing more accessible to the public.

On January 3, 2019, Ocasio-Cortez and other incoming members of the 116th Congress took the oath of office. Placing her hand on a Bible held by her mother, Blanca, Ocasio-Cortez repeated the oath administered by Speaker of the House Nancy Pelosi and promised to "support and defend the Constitution of the United States against all enemies, foreign and domestic." Afterward, Ocasio-Cortez recalled, "The Speaker said to [Blanca] 'you must be so proud,' and my mother began to cry" (Igoe 2019). Several other members of Ocasio-Cortez's family also attended the ceremony, including her brother, Gabriel, and her partner, Riley Roberts.

Some members of the historically diverse class of incoming lawmakers wore outfits to the swearing-in ceremony that represented certain aspects of their background, identity, or culture. Ocasio-Cortez chose a white suit with gold hoop earrings and her trademark red lipstick. Supporters of the women's suffrage movement in the early twentieth century often wore white to symbolize purity and femininity, and several female politicians also donned the color at key moments in their careers. Shirley Chisholm (D-NY) wore white when she became the first black woman elected to Congress in 1968, as did Geraldine Ferraro when she became the first female vice presidential nominee in 1984 and Hillary Clinton when she accepted the Democratic presidential nomination in 2016. "I wore all-white today to honor the women who paved the path before me, and for all the women yet to come," Ocasio-Cortez explained. "From suffragettes to Shirley Chisholm, I wouldn't be here if it wasn't for the mothers of the movement" (Fisher 2019).

Ocasio-Cortez's jewelry and makeup highlighted her Latina heritage and her Bronx style. She credited her choices to another ground-breaking daughter of Puerto Rican immigrants from the Bronx, Sonia Sotomayor, who became the first Latina justice of the U.S. Supreme Court in 2009. "Lip+hoops were inspired by Sonia Sotomayor, who was advised to wear neutral-colored nail polish to her confirmation hearings to avoid scrutiny. She kept her red nail polish," Ocasio-Cortez tweeted. "Next time someone tells Bronx girls to take off their hoops, they can just say they're dressing like a Congresswoman" (Fisher 2019).

Several other incoming female representatives selected outfits to provide visual symbols of their diverse backgrounds. Haaland, for instance, wore a traditional Pueblo dress with leather moccasins and turquoise jewelry. Omar wore a brightly colored hijab. Tlaib wore an embroidered Palestinian thobe and took her oath of office on a centuries-old Quran that had once belonged to Thomas Jefferson. "We should embrace who we are and not be shamed for it," Tlaib said. "Too often in this country, recently and throughout history, groups of people have been marginalized, harmed, and even killed for being different. This must change, and we can change this together" (Feller 2019).

THE BLUE WAVE

Political analysts described the Democratic gains in the 2018 midterm elections as a "blue wave," referring to the color typically used to represent the party on electoral maps. Democrats needed to pick up 24 seats in the 435-member House to take majority control of the chamber for the first time since 2010, and they did so comfortably with a net gain of 40 seats. Even more impressive was Democratic candidates' historic 8.6-point lead in the popular vote total—the widest margin ever recorded for a minority party—which equated to ten million more votes for House Democrats than House Republicans. "This wasn't just a blue wave in the House," wrote CNN analyst Harry Enten. "It was a tsunami" (Enten 2018).

Analysts mentioned many possible contributing factors to the blue wave, including Republican President Donald Trump's low approval ratings, the retirement of several key Republican incumbents, the vulnerability of two dozen Republican seats in districts carried by Democrat Hillary Clinton in the 2016 presidential election, and a Democratic base energized by the anti-Trump resistance movement. Exit polls showed that health care ranked among the most pressing issues for voters. Whereas most Democrats campaigned on protecting the coverage offered under the Affordable Care Act, many Republicans sought to repeal the law.

Political commentators debated about whether the blue wave would lead to further Democratic gains in 2020 and beyond. Some pointed out that the majority party usually lost seats in midterm elections and said flipping the House did not necessarily predict future success for the Democrats. Others argued that the midterm results reflected demographic shifts that might tend to favor Democrats for years to come. For instance, turnout among younger voters increased significantly from 2014 to 2018, from 20 percent to 36 percent for voters between ages 18 and 29, and from 36 percent to 49 percent for voters between ages 30 and 44. Democratic candidates won the support of 61 percent of these newly energized younger voters, compared to 36 percent who voted for Republican candidates (Gaudiano 2018). "There was no effort to appeal to anyone outside of the normal base," Republican strategist Rory Cooper said of his party. "The more you win in the short term, the more you can put off fixing long-term structural issues, like the age, race, and gender of the typical Republican voter" (Siddiqui 2018).

FURTHER READING

Buncombe, Andrew. 2019. "AOC Reveals Her Post-It Wall of Thank You Notes in Congress." Independent, February 12, 2019. https://www.independent.co.uk/news/world/americas/us-politics/

aoc-congress-thank-you-messages-alexandria-ocasio-cortez-post-it-notes-twitter-a8776356.html.

Cadigan, Hilary. 2018. "Alexandria Ocasio-Cortez Learned Her Most Important Lessons from Restaurants." *Bon Appetit*, November 7, 2018. https://www.yahoo.com/lifestyle/alexandria-ocasio-cortez-learned-her-141500873.html.

Castillo, Monica. 2019. "AOC Surprises Audience with Video Chat after Thrilling Sundance Premiere of *Knock Down the House*." *Remezcla*, January 31, 2019. https://remezcla.com/film/alexandria-ocasio-cortez-surprise-knock-down-the-house-sundance-premiere/.

Clark, Dartunorro. 2018. "Ocasio-Cortez Rips Fox News for Mocking Her Personal Finances, Working-Class People." NBC News, November 9, 2018. https://www.nbcnews.com/politics/politics-news/ocasio-cortez-rips-fox-news-mocking-her-personal-finances-working-n934651.

Edmondson, Catie, and Jasmine C. Lee. 2019. "Meet the New Freshmen in Congress." *The New York Times*, January 3, 2019. https://www.nytimes.com/interactive/2018/11/28/us/politics/congress-freshman-class.html?mtrref=undefined.

Enten, Harry. 2018. "Latest House Results Confirm 2018 Wasn't a Blue Wave. It Was a Blue Tsunami." CNN, December 6, 2018. https://www.cnn.com/2018/12/06/politics/latest-house-vote-blue-wave/index.html.

Feller, Madison. 2019. "Why Alexandria Ocasio-Cortez Wore All White at Her Swearing-In Ceremony." *Elle*, January 4, 2019. https://www.elle.com/culture/career-politics/a25747744/alexandria-ocasio-cortez-wore-white-swearing-in-suffragette-movement/.

Fisher, Lauren A. 2019. "Alexandria Ocasio-Cortez's Swearing-In Outfit Was a Nod to Suffragettes and Bronx Girls." *Harper's Bazaar*, January 4, 2019. https://www.harpersbazaar.com/culture/politics/a25751699/alexandria-ocasio-cortez-white-suit-congress/.

Gaudiano, Nicole. 2018. "New 'Year of the Woman'? Over 100 Female Candidates Set to Win Seats in Congress, Make History." *USA Today*, November 6, 2018. https://www.usatoday.com/story/news/politics/elections/2018/11/06/women-candidates-midterms/1845639002/.

Igoe, Katherine J. 2019. "Who Is Blanca Ocasio-Cortez, Alexandria Ocasio-Cortez's Mom?" *Marie Clarie*, January 30, 2019. https://www.marieclaire.com/politics/a26099099/who-is-alexandria-ocasio-cortez-mom-blanca/.

Johnson, Jake. 2018. "Ocasio-Cortez and Tlaib Expose Congressional Orientation's Corporate Sponsors." Truthout, December 8, 2018. https://truthout.org/articles/newly-elected-members-of-congress-expose-their-corporate-orientation/.

Madhani, Aamer, and Deborah Barfield Berry. 2018. "First Native American, Muslim Women Elected to Congress amid Minority Wins." *USA Today*, November 7, 2018. https://www.usatoday.com/story/news/politics/elections/2018/11/06/candidates-color-midterms/1839962002/.

Newell, Jim. 2018. "Here's Who Spoke at Harvard's Controversial Orientation for New Members of Congress." Slate, December 7, 2018. https://slate.com/news-and-politics/2018/12/harvard-ori entation-alexandria-ocasio-cortez-rashida-tlaib.html.

Relman, Eliza. 2018a. "Alexandria Ocasio-Cortez and Other New Progressives Are Tweeting Their Dissatisfaction with Orientation at Harvard." Business Insider, December 6, 2018. https://www.busi nessinsider.com/alexandria-ocasio-cortez-and-house-freshmen-are-protesting-orientation-harvard-2018-12.

Relman, Eliza. 2018b. "'This Is a Disgrace': Alexandria Ocasio-Cortez Slams Her Future Colleagues in Congress for Employing Unpaid Interns and Failing to Pay Staffers a 'Living Wage.'" Business Insider, December 4, 2018. https://www.businessinsider.com/alexandria-ocasio-cortez-slams-future-colleagues-congress-for-employing-unpaid-interns-living-wage-2018–12.

Siddiqui, Sabrina. 2018. "The Democratic Blue Wave Was Real." *Guardian*, November 17, 2018. https://www.theguardian.com/us-news/2018/nov/16/the-democratic-blue-wave-was-real.

Stein, Jeff. 2019. "'Here's the System; It Sucks': Meet the Staffers Hired by Ocasio-Cortez to Upend Washington." *The Washington Post*, February 14, 2019. https://www.washingtonpost.com/us-policy/2019/02/14/heres-system-it-sucks-meet-hill-staffers-ocasio-cortez-has-tapped-upend-washington.

Wanshel, Elyse. 2018. "Alexandria Ocasio-Cortez Is Totally Geeking Out while Visiting the U.S. Capitol." *Huffington Post*, November 15, 2018. https://www.huffpost.com/entry/alexandria-ocasio-cortez-is-totally-geeking-out-while-visiting-the-us-capital_n_5bec6c21e4b0598443d3b6d9.

Chapter 8

FRESHMAN LEGISLATOR

Let's say I'm only in Congress for two years. If we can radically change the conversation, then we can potentially accomplish more in two years than many people are able to shape the conversation in ten. (Cooper 2019)

Alexandria Ocasio-Cortez faced an unusual level of scrutiny as she took office as a member of the U.S. House of Representatives in January 2019. Whereas most freshman legislators fly under the national radar while they settle in and learn the ropes, Ocasio-Cortez's every move and utterance generated intense debate from her first day on the job. "She's been described as both an inspiring and idealistic insurgent, and as a naïve and ill-informed newcomer—as the future of the Democratic party, and as a potential obstacle to its success," said CBS News correspondent Anderson Cooper. "Few rookie members of Congress have put such bold ideas on the national agenda and stirred up so much controversy before they were sworn in" (Cooper 2019).

Ocasio-Cortez's status as the best-known incoming legislator yielded many opportunities during her first weeks in office. She sat down for a full-length interview for the prime-time CBS News program

60 Minutes, for instance, and she was a featured speaker at a Women's March event in New York City. Ocasio-Cortez also appeared at a ceremony honoring the birth of Martin Luther King Jr., where journalist Ta-Nehisi Coates praised her for upholding the civil rights leader's legacy of radical activism. "People called Martin Luther King divisive in his time. We forget that he was wildly unpopular when he was advocating for the Civil Rights Act," Ocasio-Cortez stated. "And I think that what we need to really realize is that social movements are the moral compass—and should be the moral compass—of our politics" (Stracqualursi 2019).

FACING PUSHBACK FROM ESTABLISHED DEMOCRATS

Since Ocasio-Cortez was elected as an antiestablishment, progressive activist, she naturally gravitated toward fellow freshmen lawmakers who expressed similar priorities, such as Ayanna Pressley, Ilhan Omar, and Rashida Tlaib. Ocasio-Cortez and her likeminded colleagues hoped to push the Democratic Party leftward to embrace the progressive policies they had promoted in their campaigns. "My personal opinion, and I know that my district and my community feel this way as well, is that we as a party have compromised too much, and we've lost too much of who we're supposed to be and who we are," Ocasio-Cortez stated (Cooper 2019).

Some moderate Democrats expressed frustration at the suggestion that inexperienced legislators could simply walk into Congress and overhaul the political system. They argued that Ocasio-Cortez and other newly elected progressives needed to move slowly, pay their dues, and build public support and political coalitions around their policy goals. When asked what advice he would give to the young woman who had defeated him in the primary, former congressman Joseph Crowley replied, "Don't come here thinking you're going to change the world overnight" (Schwartz 2019).

Critics noted that Ocasio-Cortez represented one of the most diverse and reliably liberal districts in the country, which put her in a much safer position than Democratic lawmakers who had to fight to hold their seats against strong Republican challengers. Some centrists urged the progressives to focus on expanding the Democratic congressional majority in 2020—by making incremental changes that appealed to moderate swing voters—rather than pursuing an extreme agenda at the expense of party unity. "If the next two years is just a race to offer increasingly unrealistic proposals," said Senator Chris Coons (D-DE), "it'll be difficult for us to make a credible case we should be allowed to govern again" (Cooper 2019).

Ocasio-Cortez and her staff, however, assessed the situation differently. They argued that Democrats had lost the 2016 presidential election by failing to present a bold vision for the future that energized voters. They viewed progressive ideas and organizing as the key to the party's future success. Ocasio-Cortez's chief of staff, Saikat Chakrabarti, said his goal for the congresswoman's two-year term was "to basically show the American people what will be possible if the Democrats win the House, the Senate, and the presidency in 2020, and that means putting our best foot forward. It means putting the most ambitious, the boldest, the biggest things we can, and then just build a movement around that" (Kulkarni 2018).

Ocasio-Cortez thus found herself in an interesting position as a freshman legislator. The media attention she received made her a national figure and a leader of the progressive movement. "No lawmaker in recent memory has translated so few votes into so much political and social capital so quickly," Charlotte Alter wrote in *Time* (Alter 2019). By the time she took office, Ocasio-Cortez had collected 3.5 million followers on Twitter—more than all other freshmen lawmakers combined, and surpassing even the 2.5 million followers of the top-ranking House Democrat, Nancy Pelosi. Yet while Ocasio-Cortez wielded more power than most incoming members, she still had to build relationships with her colleagues and work within the system to pass legislation. "She has as much influence outside of Congress as anybody else she serves with. Her every tweet is a potential news cycle," wrote Ryan Grim of the Intercept. "She has used that platform to shift the broader political conversation in ways previously unthinkable. . . . But inside the building, she is heavily outgunned" (Grim 2019).

Ocasio-Cortez recognized the challenges of her position. "We're going into the lion's den, even within the party," she acknowledged (Paybarah 2018). She remained committed to promoting the progressive ideas that resonated with her constituents, however, and expressed confidence in her ability to work collaboratively with her colleagues. "I think the truth of what I am is a consensus builder. And I like to think that I'm persuasive, and so I think a lot of that work is going to be on building relationships and trying to persuade and talk to my colleagues on building a progressive agenda for the party," she explained. "I genuinely do not think of politics in the world in terms of enemies or allies, or, like, permanent enemies or permanent allies. I also think of things in terms of issues, and I always think, what is our goal? What are we trying to accomplish, and who has aligned interests in getting that one thing done?" (Cooper 2019).

TUSSLING WITH HOUSE LEADERSHIP

One of the first intra-party conflicts Ocasio-Cortez faced upon taking office involved selecting House leaders. Since the Democrats had regained a majority in the 435-member House in the 2018 midterms, party members got to elect a speaker to preside over the body and set its legislative agenda. Pelosi, who had become the first female Speaker of the House during the last period of Democratic control (2007–2011), quickly emerged as the leading candidate. She needed to secure 213 votes from among 235 Democratic members to reclaim the speakership. Given Ocasio-Cortez's high-profile position among progressives, many observers waited to see whether she would endorse Pelosi's bid.

Questions regarding Ocasio-Cortez's support arose shortly after the 2018 election, when the newly elected representative participated in a climate-change protest outside Pelosi's congressional office. She joined an estimated 200 progressive activists from such organizations as the Sunrise Movement and Justice Democrats who demanded that House Democrats put forth a comprehensive plan to combat global warming. The protest called attention to a United Nations report warning that the catastrophic effects of climate change would become irreversible if the world did not take urgent action within twelve years. "Nancy Pelosi and the Democratic Party leadership must get serious about the climate and our economy," said Waleed Shahid of Justice Democrats. "Anything less is tantamount to denying the reality of climate change. The hopeful part is that we're ushering in a new generation of leaders into the Democratic Party who understand the urgency and will help build a movement to create the political will for bold action" (Segers 2018).

Some Republican lawmakers and conservative media outlets expressed surprise that a newly elected Democratic representative would join a demonstration targeting the presumptive party leader. "Huh, well this is unconventional," said AshLee Strong, spokesperson for outgoing Republican Speaker Paul Ryan. "The incoming speaker is getting protested by one of her freshmen" (Gaudiano 2018). Ocasio-Cortez insisted that her presence at the protest was not intended as a rebuke of Pelosi. She expressed admiration for the Democratic leader as someone who came from "a space of activism and organizing" and "really appreciates civic engagement" (Gaudiano 2018). Ocasio-Cortez claimed that she only wanted to amplify the voices of the protesters in calling for a concrete plan to switch the country to 100 percent renewable energy. "This is not about me, this is not about the dynamics of any personalities," she stated. "What I hope we show is that this is an encouragement of [Pelosi] and that we're here to back up bold action" (Gaudiano 2018).

Pelosi, who was not in her office at the time, responded to the demonstrations with a statement saying that she welcomed the protesters' input and supported their right to organize. "We are inspired by the energy and activism of the many young activists and advocates leading the way on the climate crisis, which threatens the health, economic security, and futures of all our communities," she said (Segers 2018). Pelosi also promised to create a select committee to address the climate crisis. Yet she minimized the influence that Ocasio-Cortez and other newly elected progressive Democrats would have over the direction of the party. "By and large, whatever orientation they came to Congress with, they know that we have to hold the center, that we have to go down the mainstream," Pelosi stated. "We must win. When we win, and we have the White House and we have [the Senate], then we can expand our exuberances to some other things" (Newell 2019).

Although Pelosi faced some opposition in her bid for the speakership, she ultimately pulled together enough support to win the position. Prior to the vote, Pelosi's allies circulated a letter praising her record of legislative accomplishments. "Now that we are faced with unprecedented threats to our democracy, women, minorities, and even the most basic American values by President Trump, we need your effective leadership more than ever to advance our efforts to help hard-working families get ahead," the letter stated (LeBlanc 2018). Ocasio-Cortez announced her intention to vote for Pelosi on Twitter. "All the challenges to Leader Pelosi are coming from her right, in an apparent effort to make the party even more conservative and bent toward corporate interests. Hard pass," she wrote. "So long as Leader Pelosi remains the most progressive candidate for Speaker, she can count on my support" (LeBlanc 2018). After Pelosi formally became speaker, Ocasio-Cortez and fellow progressives Ilhan Omar and Jahana Hayes participated in a show of party unity by appearing with Pelosi on a *Rolling Stone* magazine cover depicting "women shaping the future."

UTILIZING HER LEVERAGE

Ocasio-Cortez and other members of the 116th Congress took their seats in the midst of a federal government shutdown that began on December 22, 2018. During debate over the appropriations bill to fund government operations for 2019, President Trump demanded that Congress approve $5.7 billion to construct a wall along the southern border with Mexico to prevent migrants from entering the United States. The outgoing Republican-controlled House passed a spending bill that did not include border-wall funding, but Majority Leader Mitch McConnell (R-KY) refused to bring it to a vote in the Senate because Trump vowed to veto it. When the deadline for passing appropriations legislation passed, federal departments and agencies that provided non-essential services were forced to shut down operations, affecting 800,000 employees as well as millions of Americans who utilized government services.

Ocasio-Cortez and several other freshmen lawmakers staged a protest intended to draw attention to the effects of the government shutdown and generate public pressure on McConnell to allow a Senate vote on the House appropriations bill. They wrote a letter demanding action and set out to hand-deliver it to McConnell, chronicling their search for the majority leader on social media using the hashtag #Wheres-Mitch. After stopping by McConnell's office, the Senate library, and other spots on Capitol Hill, Ocasio-Cortez and her House colleagues took the attention-grabbing step of walking onto the floor of the Senate. "House members entering the Senate chamber is a rare occurrence, most people working in the Senate never see it happen, most staff members never see that happen," said MSNBC anchor Lawrence O'Donnell. "In modern politics—in social media politics—with fame comes power, the power to direct media attention where you want it. The power to push a policy position into the national political debate. And Congresswoman Ocasio-Cortez did that today more effectively than any other member of the House of Representatives could have done it, because of that fame" (Brigham 2019).

Ocasio-Cortez also made the government shutdown the topic of her first speech as a member of Congress. On January 16, she took to the House floor to describe a phone call she received from one of her constituents, a federal employee who worked as an air-traffic controller at John F. Kennedy International Airport in New York City. Ocasio-Cortez related how the shutdown forced the man to work without pay, adding concerns about supporting his family to the everyday stresses of his job. She placed responsibility for the shutdown squarely on Trump. "It is actually not about a wall, it is not about the border, and it is certainly not about the well-being of everyday Americans. The truth is, this shutdown is about the erosion of American democracy and the subversion of our most basic governmental norms," she stated. "Each and every member of this body has a responsibility to this nation and to everyone in the United States of America, whether they voted for us or not. And this president shares in that responsibility as well, which means he has a responsibility to my constituent" (Gajanan 2019).

C-SPAN, the television network that provides live coverage of the proceedings of Congress, recorded her four-minute speech and posted the video on Twitter. It quickly set a new record as the network's most-watched Twitter video of remarks by a House member, receiving 1.16 million views within twelve hours. Within twenty-four hours, the video had garnered 13,000 retweets and 46,000 likes (Gajanan 2019), and it eventually surpassed 3.34 million views (Schwartz 2019). The government shutdown remained in place until January 25, when growing public pressure and sagging approval ratings convinced Trump to relent on his demand for full border-wall funding.

As soon as the shutdown ended, Ocasio-Cortez became embroiled in a controversy involving the interests of people in her district. After soliciting proposals from many large cities, the giant online retailer Amazon announced plans to locate a second headquarters (HQ2) in the Queens borough of New York City. Proponents of the deal, including New York governor Andrew Cuomo and New York City mayor Bill de Blasio (both Democrats), claimed that it would provide significant economic benefits by creating 25,000 high-paying jobs and expanding the city's tax base. Opponents, including former New York City mayor Michael Bloomberg and several members of the city council, argued that the $1.5 billion in tax incentives and subsidies the city offered to attract Amazon amounted to corporate charity. Ocasio-Cortez emerged as a vocal critic of the proposed HQ2 arrangement. "Amazon is a billion-dollar company," she tweeted. "The idea that it will receive hundreds of millions of dollars in tax breaks at a time when our subway is crumbling and our communities need MORE investment, not less, is extremely concerning to residents" (Hess 2019).

On February 14, Amazon released a statement saying that it decided not to move forward with its plans to locate HQ2 in Queens because "a number of state and local politicians have made it clear that they oppose our presence" (Hess 2019). Ocasio-Cortez celebrated the news, presenting it as a victory for ordinary citizens. "Today was the day a group of dedicated, everyday New Yorkers and their neighbors defeated Amazon's corporate greed, its worker exploitation, and the power of the richest man in the world [Amazon founder Jeff Bezos]," she tweeted (Hess 2019). Since polls showed that more than half of New York City residents supported the Amazon deal, while only one-fourth opposed it, some observers predicted that Ocasio-Cortez's role in the company's decision to withdraw the planned HQ2 from the city would harm her politically. In fact, some political opponents argued that it might make the freshman legislator vulnerable to a primary challenge in 2020.

WORKING WITH HOUSE COMMITTEES

As part of the process of allocating positions and responsibilities among party members, Ocasio-Cortez received two committee assignments. On January 15, she became a member of the House Financial Services

Committee, chaired by Representative Maxine Waters (D-CA), which oversees such elements of the financial sector as banking, lending, insurance, and the stock market. "Personally, I'm looking forward to digging into the student loan crisis, examining for-profit prisons/ICE detention, and exploring the development of public and postal banking. To start," Ocasio-Cortez said (Cole 2019). On January 22, Ocasio-Cortez became a member of the House Oversight and Reform Committee, chaired by Representative Elijah Cummings (D-MD), which oversees the functioning of the federal government and has broad powers to investigate fraud and waste.

In early February, Ocasio-Cortez participated in her first congressional hearing as a member of the Financial Services Committee. She and other representatives took turns questioning a panel of ethics experts from campaign finance watchdog groups. Ocasio-Cortez used her allotted time to delve into the federal regulations guiding how political candidates and officeholders raise and spend money. She used a fictional scenario to demonstrate how current campaign finance rules, which allow unlimited donations by corporate political action committees, facilitate corruption in politics.

Ocasio-Cortez asked the panel to imagine that she was a "bad guy" seeking to "enrich myself and advance my interest, even if that means putting that ahead of the American people" (Wyatt 2019). She then outlined a series of actions that included collecting campaign donations from wealthy corporations and special interest groups, using the money to make hush payments to prevent unsavory information from becoming public, and using her elected office to reward her donors and enrich herself. The panelists confirmed that each action she described was legal under current campaign finance rules. "Now I'm elected I have the power to draft, lobby, and shape the laws that govern the USA. I can be totally funded by oil and gas, by big pharma, and there's no limit to that whatsoever," Ocasio-Cortez concluded. "We have a system right now which is fundamentally broken" (Wyatt 2019). Footage of her remarks at the hearing received 37.5 million views on the left-leaning online news site NowThis.

At the end of February, Ocasio-Cortez played a prominent role in the Oversight Committee's investigation into allegations of tax evasion, insurance fraud, illegal payoffs, and other financial wrongdoing by Trump and his 2016 presidential campaign. She and other members took turns questioning Michael Cohen, Trump's former personal attorney and "fixer," about his knowledge of the president's personal finances and business dealings. "She asked one question at a time, avoided long-winded speeches on why she was asking the question, and listened carefully to his answer, which gave her the basis for a follow-up inquiry," wrote Caroline Fredrickson of the American Constitution Society, a progressive legal organization. "As a result, Mr. Cohen gave specific answers about Mr. Trump's shady practices, along with a road map for how to find out more" (Fredrickson 2019).

Several analysts noted that Ocasio-Cortez's questioning established a legal basis for Congress to gain access to Trump's tax returns. Throughout the 2016 campaign, Trump had disregarded the precedent established by previous presidential candidates by refusing to make his tax information public. During the hearing, Cohen testified that Trump inflated the value of his assets for insurance purposes to gain favorable rates and deflated the value of his assets for tax purposes to reduce his property-tax bill. Ocasio-Cortez responded by asking, "Would it help for the committee to obtain federal and state tax returns from the president and his company to address that discrepancy?" (Willis 2019). Cohen agreed that Trump's tax returns would provide the information the committee sought. "By choosing to eschew theatrics in favor of asking substantive, straightforward questions, Alexandria Ocasio-Cortez provided party leadership with the strongest justification yet for using the subpoena power to get the president's tax returns," political analyst Jay Willis wrote in GQ magazine (Willis 2019).

HOUSE SPEAKER NANCY PELOSI

Alexandria Ocasio-Cortez's prominence among incoming progressive House Democrats created friction with some long-serving members of the party establishment, including Speaker Nancy Pelosi. Pelosi was born Nancy D'Alesandro in 1940 in Baltimore, Maryland. She grew up as part of a political family, with both her father and brother serving as mayor of her hometown.

After earning a degree from Trinity College in Washington, D.C., Nancy married Paul Pelosi, with whom she eventually had five children. The family moved to San Francisco, where Nancy became involved in local politics as a Democratic Party volunteer and organizer.

Pelosi joined Congress in 1987, when she was elected to represent a liberal district that included San Francisco in the U.S. House of Representatives. In 2002, she became the first female Democratic leader and emerged as a vocal opponent of Republican president George W. Bush's decision to launch a war in Iraq. When Democrats gained a majority in the 2006 midterm election, Pelosi became the first female speaker of the House. She lost the speakership in 2011 after Republicans regained a majority, but she won the position again following the Democratic blue wave in the 2018 midterms. As speaker, Pelosi led the congressional opposition to Republican president Donald Trump's border wall, which created an impasse that led to a thirty-five-day government shutdown.

By the time Ocasio-Cortez took office, Pelosi had been the top-ranking House Democrat for seventeen years. Some progressives viewed her as a symbol of the old-school Democratic establishment blocking their efforts to steer the party leftward. Fueling rumors of a split within the party, Pelosi made headlines in the first few months of the 116th Congress for making statements that minimized Ocasio-Cortez's influence. When one interviewer described the freshman legislator as the leader of the progressive wing of the party, Pelosi interrupted and said, "That's like five people." Clearly referring to Ocasio-Cortez, the speaker told another interviewer, "While there are people who have a large number of Twitter followers, what's important is that we have large numbers of votes on the floor of the House" (Cillizza 2019). Although Pelosi praised the energy of the newly elected progressives and insisted that their differences involved tactics rather than ideology, she also urged the newcomers to work within the system and maintain party unity.

FURTHER READING

Alter, Charlotte. 2019. "'Change Is Closer Than We Think': Inside Alexandria Ocasio-Cortez's Unlikely Rise." *Time*, March 21, 2019. http://time.com/longform/alexandria-ocasio-cortez-profile/.

Brigham, Bob. 2019. "#WheresMitch: Alexandria Ocasio-Cortez Searches for Missing in Action McConnell as Shutdown Drags On." Salon, January 17, 2019. https://www.salon.com/2019/01/17/wheresmitch-alexandria-ocasio-cortez-searches-for-missing-in-action-mcconnell-as-shutdown-drags-on_partner/.

Cillizza, Chris. 2019. "Nancy Pelosi Just Won't Stop Trolling Alexandria Ocasio-Cortez." CNN, April 15, 2019. https://www.cnn.com/2019/04/15/politics/nancy-pelosi-aoc/index.html.

Cole, Devan. 2019. "Alexandria Ocasio-Cortez Secures Seat on Powerful House Financial Services Committee." CNN, January 16, 2019. https://www.cnn.com/2019/01/16/politics/alexandria-ocasio-cortez-financial-services-committee/index.html.

Cooper, Anderson. 2019. "Alexandria Ocasio-Cortez: The Rookie Congresswoman Challenging the Democratic Establishment" [*60 Minutes* interview]. CBS News, January 6, 2019. https://www.cbsnews.com/news/alexandria-ocasio-cortez-the-rookie-congresswoman-challenging-the-democratic-establishment-60-minutes-interview-full-transcript-2019–01–06/.

Frederickson, Caroline. 2019. "How Alexandria Ocasio-Cortez Won the Cohen Hearing." *The New York Times*, February 28, 2019. https://www.nytimes.com/2019/02/28/opinion/alexandria-ocasio-cortez-cohen-hearing.html?smid=nytcore-ios-share.

Gajanan, Mahita. 2019. "Alexandria Ocasio-Cortez's First Speech Broke a C-SPAN Record." *Time*, January 18, 2019. http://time.com/5506749/alexandria-ocasio-cortezs-house-speech-cspan-record/.

Gaudiano, Nicole. 2018. "On Her First Day of Orientation on Capitol Hill, Alexandria Ocasio-Cortez Protests in Pelosi's Office." *USA Today*, November 13, 2018. https://www.usatoday.com/story/news/politics/2018/11/13/alexandria-ocasio-cortez-nancy-pelosi/1987514002/.

Grim, Ryan. 2019. "The Contradiction Ocasio-Cortez and Her Allies Will Need to Resolve." Bad News (blog), January 3, 2019. https://badnews.substack.com/p/the-contradiction-ocasio-cortez-and.

Hess, Abigail. 2019. "Alexandria Ocasio-Cortez: Amazon Abandoning Its Plans for a New York Headquarters Proves 'Anything Is Possible.'" CNBC, February 14, 2019. https://www.cnbc.com/2019/02/14/ocasio-cortez-amazon-cancelling-nyc-hq-proves-anything-is-possible.html.

Kulkarni, Bhargavi. 2018. "Saikat Chakrabarti: The Techie behind Alexandria Ocasio-Cortez." India Abroad, December 16, 2018. https://www.indiaabroad.com/indian-americans/saikat-chakrabarti-the-techie-behind-alexandria-ocasio-cortez/article_7524 0282-0187-11e9-a432–93f98a2205ce.html.

LeBlanc, Paul. 2018. "Ocasio-Cortez Backs Pelosi for Speaker as Long as She 'Remains the Most Progressive Candidate.'" CNN, November 22, 2018. https://www.cnn.com/2018/11/21/politics/alexandria-ocasio--cortez-nancy-pelosi-house-speaker/index .html.

Newell, Jim. 2019. "Why Nancy Pelosi Is So Comfortable Dismissing the Influence of AOC and Her Fellow Lefties." Slate, April 15, 2019. https://slate.com/news-and-politics/2019/04/nancy-pelosi-aoc-lefties-congress.html.

Paybarah, Azi. 2018. "Alexandria Ocasio-Cortez Will Push Washington. Will Washington Push Back?" The New York Times, November 7, 2018. https://www.nytimes.com/2018/11/07/nyregion/ocasio-cortez-congress-washington.html.

Schwartz, Hunter. 2019. "Alexandria Ocasio-Cortez's First Month in Office: A List." CNN, February 3, 2019. https://www.cnn.com/2019/02/03/politics/alexandria-ocasio-cortez-aoc-first-month-in-congress/index.html.

Segers, Grace. 2018. "Alexandria Ocasio-Cortez Participates in Protest outside Nancy Pelosi's Office." CBS News, November 13, 2018. https://www.cbsnews.com/news/alexandria-ocasio-cortez-participates-in-protest-outside-nancy-pelosi-office/.

Stracqualursi, Veronica. 2019. "Colbert Asks How Many 'F—s' Ocasio-Cortez Gives about Dem Criticism. Her Response: 'Zero.'" CNN,

January 22, 2019. https://www.cnn.com/2019/01/22/politics/aoc-stephen-colbert-interview-zero/index.html.

Willis, Jay. 2019. "Alexandria Ocasio-Cortez Asked the Sharpest Questions in the Michael Cohen Hearing." *GQ*, February 28, 2019. https://www.gq.com/story/aoc-cohen-hearing.

Wyatt, Tim. 2019. "Alexandria Ocasio-Cortez Delivers Devastating Dissection of U.S. Financial System and Political Corruption in Congress Speech." *Independent*, February 8, 2019. https://www.independent.co.uk/news/world/americas/us-politics/alexandria-ocasio-cortez-congress-speech-campaign-finance-corruption-election-aoc-a8769381.html.

Chapter 9

CONSERVATIVE BACKLASH

It feels like an extra job. I've got a full-time job in Congress and then I moonlight as America's greatest villain, or as the new hope. And it's pretty tiring. I'm just a normal person. (Remnick 2019)

The attention Alexandria Ocasio-Cortez received in the media—and the praise she received from progressives—generated a massive backlash among conservatives. Republican lawmakers, conservative political analysts, right-wing pundits, and members of the Trump family all weighed in to question, criticize, mock, and dismiss the freshman congresswoman. Some observers described her political opponents' intense focus on Ocasio-Cortez as an obsession. "Conservatives hang on her every word, waiting for her to slip, and dig through her past for any feeble sign that she isn't who she says she is," Laura Bassett wrote in the *Huffington Post*. "There's an existential, panicked tinge to the behavior here—what you might call 'AOC Derangement Syndrome'" (Bassett 2019).

An analysis by the progressive organization *Media Matters for America* found that the conservative news channels Fox News and Fox

Business mentioned Ocasio-Cortez 3,181 times—or around 75 times per day—during the six-week period between February 25 and April 7, 2019. According to *The Washington Post*, Fox News devoted more coverage to Ocasio-Cortez during her first month in Congress than it gave to any of the Democrats running for president in 2020, with the exception of Senator Elizabeth Warren (D-MA) (Beauchamp 2019). Likewise, the right-leaning *New York Post* published two dozen articles about Ocasio-Cortez in less than a week (Smith 2019). "It's astonishing that a Democratic backbencher could get this much attention and get so famous at the beginning of her first term," wrote Vox contributor Zack Beauchamp. "It's a testament to how much of a phenomenon she is on the Democratic left—and how much the right seems to both hate and fear her" (Beauchamp 2019).

Given that new legislators have little real power in a 435-member House that operates on the basis of seniority, some commentators asserted that conservative efforts to discredit Ocasio-Cortez had the opposite effect by raising her profile, both in Washington and on the national stage. "Their relentless focus on a minor member . . . has completely backfired and turned Ocasio-Cortez into one of the most recognizable members of Congress and a super hero of the progressive left with powers that far outpace her actual rank on Capitol Hill," said NBC News correspondent Matt Laslo. "She's now the talk of the town. One could even call her a titan, because lawmakers twice her age . . . are now forced to react to her ideas rather than ignore them as generations of lawmakers have ignored freshmen before her" (Laslo 2019).

On the other hand, some observers claimed that the conservative focus on Ocasio-Cortez proved effective in rallying opposition to her ideas, which sources on the political right portrayed as radical and dangerous. "Republicans would love to make her the face the Democratic party. It's from the Trump playbook: they would love to characterize the Democrats as this young, radical socialist from New York," conservative commentator Charlie Sykes explained. "Trump always needs a foil and she's a very useful foil for him to say: 'I'm running against radical socialists'" (Smith 2019). For her part, Ocasio-Cortez used the vilification and criticism as motivation to work harder to achieve meaningful change. "That's how hard they're fighting against dignified healthcare, wages, and justice for all; and turning their firepower on the youngest

Congresswoman in history to do it," she wrote on Twitter. "Too bad for them, 'cause we don't flinch" (Morrow 2019).

QUESTIONING HER BACKGROUND

Beginning shortly after her surprise victory in the Democratic primary, conservative critics raised questions about the accuracy of Ocasio-Cortez's campaign biography, which had helped the candidate forge a personal connection with voters in her diverse, working-class district. Dozens of news articles and social media posts sought to discredit elements of Ocasio-Cortez's background and history and expose her as a fraud in the eyes of her constituents. One reporter, for example, posted a photograph of Ocasio-Cortez's modest suburban childhood home on Twitter, accompanied by a message casting doubt on her Bronx roots. "This is the Yorktown Heights (very nice area) home @Ocasio2018 grew up in before going off to Ivy League Brown University," tweeted John Cardillo of Newsmax. "A far cry from the Bronx hood upbringing she's selling" (Da Silva 2019).

Ocasio-Cortez immediately corrected Cardillo by noting that she had attended Boston University—which is not an Ivy League institution—rather than Brown. She also restated how her experiences going back and forth between Yorktown Heights and the Bronx had provided a first-hand look at the impacts of economic inequality. "My mom scrubbed toilets so I could live here," she noted. "And I grew up seeing how the ZIP code one is born in determines much of their opportunity" (Da Silva 2019). When asked why she bothered responding to such insinuations, Ocasio-Cortez said she was unwilling to back down to bullies. "I'm not going to let some clown that's never stepped in the Bronx tell me about my relationship to the Bronx. Get out of here," she stated. "He was trying to strip me of the fact that I'm a third-generation Bronxite. He was trying to cast doubt on who I am, where my family is from" (Feller 2018).

Ocasio-Cortez also came under criticism for saying that she would have trouble affording an apartment in Washington, D.C., until she started collecting her paycheck as a member of Congress. When Ocasio-Cortez eventually signed a lease in a high-rise building where rents ranged up to $5,000 per month, conservative critics called her a liar and a hypocrite, even though many legislators lived in far more upscale settings. The controversy surrounding Ocasio-Cortez's housing arrangements irritated the congresswoman's mother, Blanca, who insisted that her daughter's position required a basic level of security and privacy. "She told me she picked that building because the amenities allow her not to get out that much. There's a gym and yoga on the premises," Blanca explained. "When she is out and about, she gets stopped every minute" (Lambiet 2019).

Much of the criticism directed toward Ocasio-Cortez focused on her wardrobe. Many detractors claimed that she dressed too well for a former bartender who claimed to have struggled financially. In September 2018, for instance, Ocasio-Cortez posed for an *Interview* magazine photo shoot wearing a $3,000 green suit by designer Gabriela Hearst and $600 black shoes by designer Manolo Blahnik. Charlie Kirk, founder of the conservative student group Turning Point USA, declared it inappropriate for someone "who pretends to be a champion of the people" to wear such an expensive outfit "while saying the rich have too much power and that socialism hasn't been tried" (Del Valle 2018). Conservative commentator Katie Pavlich echoed these sentiments, telling *Fox and Friends* that "the rising star of the Democratic Party has expensive tastes for a socialist" and joking that Ocasio-Cortez should redistribute wealth by handing over the designer shoes (Del Valle 2018). Ocasio-Cortez responded by pointing out that *Interview* borrowed the clothing she wore in the photo shoot, and that she did not get to keep the outfit.

Two months later, as Ocasio-Cortez prepared to take office, *Washington Examiner* writer Eddie Scarry tweeted a photo of the freshman legislator walking down a Capitol hallway and offered commentary on her outfit. "I'll tell you something: that jacket and coat don't look like a girl who struggles," he wrote (Da Silva 2019). Scarry later attempted to clarify the statement, saying that he intended to compliment Ocasio-Cortez for looking "well put together—ELEGANT even—despite suggestions she's struggled" (Del Valle 2018). Many progressive commentators remarked on Scarry's insinuation that people from working-class backgrounds could not dress professionally. "The underlying message here is that if working people own anything beyond the bare minimum, then they're not really struggling," wrote Vox contributor

Gaby Del Valle. "It points to a culture in which people who can't afford things like health care or housing are blamed for their inability to do so, instead of the blame falling on the policies, and politicians, that make health care and housing so expensive in the first place" (Del Valle 2018).

INSULTING HER INTELLIGENCE

Much of the criticism aimed at Ocasio-Cortez questioned her intellect. Detractors often portrayed her as an inexperienced, uninformed political lightweight who lacked the ability to grasp complicated policy issues. Right-wing commentator Dinesh D'Souza described the freshman congresswoman as "the stupidest person elected to public office," for instance, while the conservative radio personalities known as Chicks on the Right added, "We're talking full-blown dumb-dumb" (Da Silva 2019). Fox News host Tucker Carlson made a variety of derogatory statements about Ocasio-Cortez, referring to her as an "idiot wind bag," a "pompous little twit," and a "moron and nasty and more self-righteous than any televangelist" (Associated Press 2019). After White House counselor Kellyanne Conway told Fox News that Ocasio-Cortez "doesn't seem to know much about anything," the congresswoman responded by tweeting, "Leveraging those who belittle my capacity is exactly how I defeated a multi-generation, multi-million $ political machine. GOP is even weaker because their bias has no self-control" (Da Silva 2019).

Shortly before the November election, Ocasio-Cortez misspoke when answering a reporter's question about the Democrats' chances of regaining control of Congress. When she referred to the "three chambers of government" and "three chambers of Congress," critics quickly pointed out that the U.S. government has three branches (executive, legislative, and judicial), while the U.S. Congress has two chambers (the Senate and House). One of the most prominent Republicans to call attention to the gaffe was Sarah Palin, the former governor of Alaska and the running mate of Senator John McCain during his unsuccessful 2008 presidential campaign. "YIKES," Palin tweeted. "Ocasio-Cortez Fumbles Basic Civics TWICE." Dozens of Twitter users noted the irony of Palin—who made a number of famous misstatements during her vice presidential run—criticizing someone else's verbal error. Ocasio-Cortez advised her political opponents to focus on policy debates. "Maybe instead of Republicans drooling over every minute of footage of me in slow-mo, waiting to chop up word slips that I correct in real-time, they actually step up enough to make the argument they want to make: that they don't believe people deserve a right to healthcare," she tweeted (Mazza 2018).

In January, an anonymous Twitter user posted a video clip of a young Ocasio-Cortez dancing on a rooftop. The poster made it clear that the footage was intended to embarrass the congresswoman and make her look foolish, describing it derisively as a "high school video of 'Sandy' Ocasio-Cortez" and noting, "Here is America's favorite commie know-it-all acting like the clueless nitwit she is" (Da Silva 2019). Ocasio-Cortez shot the video with friends in 2009, during her years as an undergraduate at Boston University. It reflected a cultural trend at that time in which college students set the dance scenes from popular 1980s "Brat Pack" movies to the song "Lisztomania" by the French band Phoenix. In her video, Ocasio-Cortez re-created the role played by actress Ally Sheedy in the iconic 1985 film *The Breakfast Club*.

The attempt to humiliate Ocasio-Cortez backfired. Although the video went viral online—receiving more than twenty-two million views around the world (Goldmacher 2019)—most viewers found it charming and delightful. "Cannot wait for my enemies to post a video of me spinning around looking super hot with the shiny hair of youth and act like they just caught me breaking into the Watergate Hotel," journalist Nicole Cliffe wrote (Lang 2019). Thousands of Twitter users praised the freshman legislator's exuberant dance moves and defended her right to have fun in college. She even received kudos from Sheedy, her costar Molly Ringwald, and members of Phoenix. Ocasio-Cortez responded to the uproar by posting a new video that showed her boogying outside her Capitol office. "I hear the GOP thinks women dancing are scandalous," she tweeted. "Wait till they find out Congresswomen dance too!" (Da Silva 2019).

Ocasio-Cortez was considerably less amused by a fake picture circulated on social media that supposedly showed the congresswoman reclining naked in a bathtub. Several conservative media outlets reposted the photo without indicating that it was fraudulent. The right-wing website The Daily Caller, for instance, included the image in a sensationalistic story titled "Here's the Photo Some People Described as a Nude Selfie of Alexandria Ocasio-Cortez." Ocasio-Cortez attributed the "completely disgusting behavior" by conservative news outlets to sexism, claiming that it proved "women in leadership face more scrutiny. Period" (Palmer 2019).

Ocasio-Cortez criticized other conservative commentators for resorting to sexist language and insults to diminish her rather than engaging in reasoned political discourse. Ed Rollins, chairman of the pro-Trump Great America PAC, referred to the congresswoman as a "little girl" on the Fox Business Network while discussing her proposal to enact a 70 percent marginal income tax rate on earnings above a certain level by the wealthiest Americans. Ocasio-Cortez posted a link to the segment on Twitter. "GOP loves to insult my intelligence, yet offers *this* as their best and most seasoned opposition to my policy proposals," she wrote. "If anything, this dude is a walking argument to tax misogyny at 100%. Republicans rob everyone the opportunity of real policy debate by resorting to this" (Moritz-Rabson 2019).

Some political opponents challenged Ocasio-Cortez's policy positions by claiming that she lacked the sophistication to analyze complex problems. Her opposition to Amazon's plan to build a second headquarters in New York City, which contributed to the tech giant's decision to withdraw from the deal, came under intense fire by her critics. New York mayor Bill DeBlasio argued that Ocasio-Cortez did not understand the details of the arrangement, while conservative pundits suggested that the congresswoman needed to "retake basic math" (Da Silva 2019). One group of detractors paid to place the message "Thanks for nothing, AOC!" on a billboard in Times Square. Ocasio-Cortez rejected the personal attacks on her intelligence and emphasized the reasoning behind her position. "Frankly, the knee-jerk reaction assuming that I 'don't understand' how tax giveaways to corps work is disappointing," she responded on Twitter. "No, it's not possible that I could come to a different conclusion. The debate *must* be over my intelligence and understanding, instead of the merits of the deal" (Da Silva 2019).

RAISING HER PROFILE

During the flurry of interviews and appearances that followed her surprise primary victory and history-making election to Congress,

Ocasio-Cortez made a number of misstatements, factual errors, exaggerations, and inconsistencies while discussing issues and policies. Mainstream media outlets and political fact-checking sites provided critical analysis of several questionable claims made by the freshman congresswoman. *The Washington Post*, CNN, and PolitiFact, for instance, pointed out inaccuracies in Ocasio-Cortez's assertions that unemployment rates were artificially low because so many Americans held multiple jobs, that continued inaction on global climate change would cause the world to end within twelve years, and that the U.S. Immigration and Customs Enforcement Agency (ICE) faced a mandate to keep 34,000 beds full of migrant detainees. "If people want to really blow up one figure here or one word there, I would argue that they're missing the forest for the trees," she said. "I think that there's a lot of people more concerned about being precisely, factually, and semantically correct than about being morally right" (Relman 2019).

Supporters argued that the intense media scrutiny surrounding Ocasio-Cortez amplified minor mistakes that might have otherwise escaped notice. "To be fair to Ocasio-Cortez," wrote *Washington Post* fact-checker Glenn Kessler, "the average member of Congress might easily make many bloopers over the course of so many live interviews" (Kessler 2018). Ocasio-Cortez encouraged critics to focus on the big-picture ideas behind her policies rather than her occasional, "rookie" mistakes in describing them. "If we want everyday, working-class Americans to run for office, and not like these robots," she stated, "we have to acknowledge and accept imperfection and growth and humanity in our government" (Minsberg 2018).

Some critics—including fellow Democrats—offered substantive criticism of the sweeping changes that Ocasio-Cortez proposed. They argued that such progressive ideas as Medicare for All, a federal jobs guarantee, free college tuition, and abolishing ICE were impractical or prohibitively expensive, and they challenged the freshman legislator to produce detailed plans for accomplishing her goals. Ocasio-Cortez also faced legitimate questions regarding delays in opening an office in her district and irregularities in the distribution of funds from her election campaign. Yet the tenor of the attacks aimed at her background, appearance, behavior, and intelligence seemed to go beyond ordinary partisan disagreements. "I knew that I was not going to be liked. I'm a Democrat. I'm a woman. I'm a *young* woman. A Latina. And I'm a liberal," Ocasio-Cortez acknowledged. "But this ravenous hysteria—it's really getting to a level that is kind of out of control. It's dangerous and even scary" (Remnick 2019).

Political observers on both the left and the right attempted to explain the apparent conservative obsession with Ocasio-Cortez. Some concluded that opponents perceive the young Latina socialist as an existential threat to the longstanding system that vests most political power in the hands of wealthy white men. "This is a millennial female minority, the three things the Fox News audience seem to fear the most," said Kurt Bardella, former spokesperson for the right-wing Breitbart News (Smith 2019). "They are obsessed with AOC because she scares the hell out of them," added Neil Sroka of the progressive group Democracy for America. "She's a young Latina woman advocating a sharp change in the policy trajectory of the country, and that's horrifying for them. It's everything they're scared of" (Smith 2019).

Some commentators argued that the conservative attacks on Ocasio-Cortez grew out of the same feelings of fear and resentment that fueled Trump's election. "During the 2016 campaign, for every problem America faced, Trump found an enemy, an outsider to blame," Adam Serwer wrote in the *Atlantic*. "Latino immigrants stealing jobs and lowering wages, Muslims engaging in terrorism, black men committing crimes." Serwer claimed that critics sought to discredit Ocasio-Cortez because "she represents the prospect of a more progressive, diverse America where those who were once deprived of power and influence can shape the course of the nation and its politics" (Serwer 2019). Caroline Heldman, a scholar in the field of gender and politics, asserted that Ocasio-Cortez threatened to upend the established sociopolitical order in many ways. "She doesn't just challenge the patriarchy," Heldman stated. "She's challenging the race, class, and gender hierarchies all at once, as well as the capitalist system that requires member of Congress be wealthy before they get there" (Bassett 2019).

Political analysts also debated about whether the disproportionate attention Ocasio-Cortez received from conservative sources had the desired effects of building opposition to her policies and limiting her effectiveness as a legislator. Some observers claimed that the barrage of spurious attacks distracted from real concerns about her political agenda.

"More substantive criticisms struggle to take root," wrote journalist Charlie Warzel, "in part because Ocasio-Cortez is quick to acknowledge missteps, but also because she's constantly moving forward, advancing her argument, tweaking the agenda, and otherwise antiquating those cable news chyrons that might seek to belittle her" (Warzel 2019). Some political opponents argued that the failed attempts to discredit the freshman congresswoman only increased her credibility. "All these lame efforts to roast Ocasio-Cortez are only making her (and socialism) look better," said Infowars editor Paul Joseph Watson (Warzel 2019).

Several polls conducted during Ocasio-Cortez's first few months in office suggested that the adverse publicity had reduced her approval ratings. A Quinnipac poll released in March 2019, for instance, found that 23 percent of Americans held a favorable view of the freshman congresswoman, while 36 percent held an unfavorable view (Beauchamp 2019). A closer examination of the data, however, revealed that her negative national opinion ratings were driven almost exclusively by Republicans. While 74 percent of Republicans viewed Ocasio-Cortez unfavorably and only 23 percent did not know enough to form an opinion, 47 percent of Democrats viewed her favorably and 44 percent were unfamiliar with her (Beauchamp 2019). "In their over-zealousness, Republicans are only serving to make her a more impactful and significant figure," Bardella said. "AOC's name ID on Fox News is absurdly high" (Smith 2019).

Ocasio-Cortez and her staff expected to encounter intense scrutiny, staunch opposition, and even personal attacks from conservative commentators and media outlets. "When a working-class person wins, when a person without a political background wins, there is going to be a backlash—you don't have experience, you don't know anything, you are dumb," said Waleed Shahid of Justice Democrats. He predicted that the negative attention would backfire by raising Ocasio-Cortez's national profile and revealing conservative biases against women, minorities, and working-class people. "The way the D.C. media and the conservative media in particular tear into AOC around being a working-class person or a person of color or a Puerto Rican, I don't think the public likes it very much," Shahid stated. "The public sees a Cinderella story, a bartender who goes against the machine and wins. And you see the way she is dragged by the D.C. establishment and the media, we lean into it, as if to say, 'If that's what they think about her, what do you think they think about you?'" (Freedlander 2019).

Some supporters argued that the conservative backlash against Ocasio-Cortez might alienate voters in certain demographic groups—especially women and minorities—and push them away from the Republican Party. Although the 116th Congress featured the most diverse group of representatives in U.S. history, most of the successful candidates who contributed to this phenomenon ran as Democrats. The record 102 women elected to the House in 2018, for instance, included 89 Democrats and only 13 Republicans. Of the 198 Republicans serving in the House, 88 percent were white men, and more than half were over age 50 (Bassett 2019). Some observers noted that the relentless conservative focus on Ocasio-Cortez might tend to perpetuate this pattern. "The way they've talked about some of the new women in the 116th Congress, and the way they've tried to belittle or mock [Ocasio-Cortez], this just makes women feel like, 'Oh, this party is not welcoming of women,'" said gender and politics scholar Laurel Elder. "'This is not a place where I'd feel comfortable throwing my hat in the ring.' Now the dynamic has a life of its own" (Bassett 2019).

DOMINATING THE NEWS CYCLE

Alexandria Ocasio-Cortez received an unprecedented amount of national press coverage—both positive and negative—for a new member of Congress. In fact, some analysts claimed that she garnered more media attention in a few short months than members of Congress typically achieved over the course of their political careers. The conservative Fox News dedicated more than 2 hours of coverage to Ocasio-Cortez's first five days in Congress, for example, while CNN spent 1.5 hours and MSNBC spent nearly an hour (Goldmacher 2019). As online media analyst Ben Thompson noted, neither Ocasio-Cortez's "background nor her position as a first-time representative are . . . noteworthy enough to be driving the national political conversation. And yet she is doing exactly that" (Rothschild and Allen 2019).

Some observers attributed the extraordinary level of attention Ocasio-Cortez received to her ability to connect with a large base of followers on social media. Axios reported that Ocasio-Cortez generated more interactions (likes and retweets) on Twitter in the weeks immediately before and after she took office than the six most prolific news sites combined. Consequently, news organizations seeking to maximize traffic on their sites, generate revenue for their advertisers, and increase profits for their shareholders were more likely to pick up social media stories by and about Ocasio-Cortez than those concerning any other Democrat (Rothschild and Allen 2019). "The congresswoman's mastery of social media has won her a massive, personal audience of extremely online millennials—whose eyeballs just happen to be more valuable to advertisers than (virtually) any other demographic's," Eric Levitz wrote in *New York* magazine. "Major news outlets haven't put 'AOC' in their spotlights because they admire her ideology, but because they covet her audience" (Levitz 2019).

Nevertheless, the extensive media attention granted to Ocasio-Cortez served to amplify her progressive platform and shift debate within the Democratic Party to the left. The freshman congresswoman's remarkable influence forced others to discuss her ideas, respond to her policy proposals, and emulate her tactics. "She absolutely does have the ability to put issues on the map," said Representative Pramila Jayapal (D-WA), leader of the Congressional Progressive Caucus. "It's not that there haven't been champions of these issues before. But when you've got [4.5] million Twitter followers and a press that will cover anything you say, it's a huge opportunity for us" (Goldmacher 2019). As Levitz put it, "The congresswoman has turned the corporate media into an agent of socialist change" (Levitz 2019).

FURTHER READING

Associated Press. 2019. "Study: Fox News Is Obsessed with Alexandria Ocasio-Cortez." *USA Today*, April 14, 2019. https://www.usatoday.com/story/life/tv/2019/04/14/study-fox-news-obsessed-alexandria-ocasio-cortez/3466493002/.

Bassett, Laura. 2019. "Conservative Men Are Obsessed with Alexandria Ocasio-Cortez. Science Tells Us Why." *Huffington Post*, January 11, 2019. https://www.huffpost.com/entry/conservatives-afraid-alexandria-ocasio-cortez_n_5c38cb74e4b05cb31c421cc3.

Beauchamp, Zack. 2019. "Conservative Media's War on AOC Is Hammering Her Poll Numbers." Vox, March 28, 2019. https://www.vox.com/policy-and-politics/2019/3/28/18285533/aoc-alexandria-ocasio-cortez-poll-favorables-media.

Da Silva, Chantal. 2019. "AOC vs. GOP: The Long List of Smears and Insults Hurled at Alexandria Ocasio-Cortez." *Newsweek*, February 21, 2019. https://www.newsweek.com/alexandria-ocasio-cortez-republicans-gop-insults-1335151.

Del Valle, Gaby. 2018. "The Real Reason Conservative Critics Love Talking about Alexandria Ocasio-Cortez's Clothes." Vox, November 16, 2018. https://www.vox.com/the-goods/2018/11/16/18099074/alexandria-ocasio-cortez-clothes-eddie-scarry.

Feller, Madison. 2018. "Alexandria Ocasio-Cortez Knows She Can't Save America All by Herself." *Elle*, July 16, 2018. https://www.elle.com/culture/career-politics/a22118408/alexandria-ocasio-cortez-interview/.

Freedlander, David. 2019. "There Is Going to Be a War within the Party. We Are Going to Lean into It." Politico, February 4, 2019. https://www.politico.com/magazine/story/2019/02/04/the-insurgents-behind-alexandria-ocasio-cortez-224542.

Goldmacher, Shane. 2019. "Ocasio-Cortez Pushes Democrats to the Left, whether They Like It or Not." *The New York Times*, January 13, 2019. https://www.nytimes.com/2019/01/13/nyregion/ocasio-cortez-democrats-congress.html.

Kessler, Glenn. 2018. "Fact Checking Alexandria Ocasio-Cortez's Media Blitz." *The Washington Post*, August 10, 2018. https://www.washingtonpost.com/news/fact-checker/wp/2018/08/10/fact-checking-alexandria-ocasio-cortezs-media-blitz.

Lambiet, Jose. 2019. "Exclusive: 'God Played Quite a Joke on Me with This Politics Stuff.'" *Daily Mail*, March 4, 2019. https://www.dailymail.co.uk/news/article-6748793/Alexandria-Ocasio-Cortezs-mother-tells-hopes-daughter-marries-longtime-boyfriend.html.

Lang, Cady. 2019. "Here's the Viral Internet Trend that Inspired that Alexandria Ocasio-Cortez Dancing Video." *Time*, January 3,

2019. https://time.com/5493430/alexandria-ocasio-cortez-danc
ing-video/.

Laslo, Matt. 2019. "AOC's Power in Washington Is Derived from the
Conservative Obsession with Her." NBC News, April 10, 2019.
https://www.nbcnews.com/think/opinion/aoc-s-power-washing
ton-derived-relentless-conservative-obsession-her-ncna992756.

Levitz, Eric. 2019. "Alexandria Ocasio-Cortez Has Turned the Corporate Media into an Agent of Social Change." New York,
January 15, 2019. http://nymag.com/intelligencer/2019/01/oca
sio-cortez-twitter-social-media-corporate-media-socialism.html.

Mazza, Ed. 2018. "Sarah Palin's Attempt to Mock Alexandria Ocasio-Cortez's 'Fumble' Backfires on Twitter." Huffington Post,
November 20, 2018. https://www.huffpost.com/entry/sarah-palin-
alexandria-ocasio-cortez_n_5bf38c4be4b0376c9e6819de.

Minsberg, Talya. 2018. "How Alexandria Ocasio-Cortez Is Bringing Her Instagram Followers into the Political Process." The
New York Times, November 16, 2018. https://www.nytimes
.com/2018/11/16/us/politics/ocasio-cortez-instagram-congress.html.

Moritz-Rabson, Daniel. 2019. "Alexandria Ocasio-Cortez Fake Nude
Photos Debunked by Foot Fetishist." Newsweek, January 7, 2019.
https://www.newsweek.com/alexandria-ocasio-cortez-fake-nude-
debunked-foot-fetishists-1282672.

Morrow, Brendan. 2019. "Fox News and Fox Business Mentioned Alexandria Ocasio-Cortez More Than 3,000 Times in 42 Days." The
Week, April 12, 2019. https://theweek.com/speedreads/834984/
fox-news-fox-business-mentioned-alexandria-ocasiocortez-
more-than-3000-times-42-days.

Palmer, Ewan. 2019. "AOC Slams 'Disgusting' Conservative Media
after Fake Nude Photo Published." Newsweek, January 10, 2019.
https://www.newsweek.com/aoc-slams-disgusting-conservative-
media-after-fake-nude-photo-published-no-1286203.

Relman, Eliza. 2019. "Alexandria Ocasio-Cortez Says She Writes All
Her Own Tweets, and Many of Them 'Never See the Light of
Day.'" Business Insider, January 7, 2019. https://www.businessin
sider.com/alexandria-ocasio-cortez-tweets-twitter-delete-2019-1.

Remnick, David. 2019. "Alexandria Ocasio-Cortez Is Coming for
Your Hamburgers!" The New Yorker, March 3, 2019. https://

www.newyorker.com/news/daily-comment/alexandria-ocasio-cortez-is-coming-for-your-hamburgers.

Rothschild, Neal, and Mike Allen. 2019. "Alexandria Ocasio-Cortez Has More Twitter Power than Media, Establishment." Axios, January 19, 2019. https://www.axios.com/ocasio-cortez-domi nates-twitter-6a997938-b8a5-4a8b-a895-0a1bcd073fea.html.

Serwer, Adam. 2019. "The Exceptions to the Rulers." *Atlantic*, January 9, 2019. https://www.theatlantic.com/ideas/archive/2019/01/why-conservatives-cant-stop-talking-about-alexandria-ocasio-cortez/579901/.

Smith, David. 2019. "AOC TMZ: Why Republicans Obsess over Alexandria Ocasio-Cortez." *Guardian*, March 31, 2019. https://www .theguardian.com/us-news/2019/mar/31/alexandria-ocasio-cortez-aoc-republicans-trump.

Sullivan, Margaret. 2019. "Alexandria Ocasio-Cortez Is Freaking Out the News Media. And It's Working for Her." *The Washington Post*, January 14, 2019. https://www.washingtonpost.com/life style/style/alexandria-ocasio-cortez-is-freaking-out-the-news-media-and-its-working-for-her/2019/01/14/.

Warzel, Charlie. 2019. "Alexandria Ocasio-Cortez Is a Perfect Foil for the Pro-Trump Media." BuzzFeed News, January 7, 2019. https://www.buzzfeednews.com/article/charliewarzel/alexand ria-ocasio-cortez-is-a-perfect-foil-for-the-pro.

Chapter 10

SOCIAL MEDIA PRESENCE

The top tip, I think, is really to be yourself and to really write your own tweets so that people know it's you talking. (Dwyer 2019)

Many analysts attributed Alexandria Ocasio-Cortez's meteoric rise in national prominence to her mastery of social media as a political tool. Throughout her primary election campaign as well as during her tenure in Congress, Ocasio-Cortez used Twitter, Instagram, and Facebook to forge personal connections with constituents and fans, inspire people to volunteer or donate money, explain and promote her policy ideas, defend herself from criticism, make the inner workings of government more transparent and accessible to voters, and raise public awareness of problems facing the country. "She is a digital native of a generation raised on social media," according to social media consultant Peter Friedman, "and a master of its language, forms, and emotional energy" (Friedman 2018). "Ocasio-Cortez wields her generational stance as a weapon," added journalist Charlie Warzel. "She's born of the internet and instinctively excels at modern political information warfare" (Warzel 2019).

As of June 2019, Ocasio-Cortez had 4.5 million followers on Twitter and 3.7 million fans on Instagram. Her Twitter following increased by 600 percent—from less than 500,000 to more than 3 million—in the eight months following her June 2018 primary victory. In December 2018, Ocasio-Cortez announced a change in her Twitter handle from @Ocasio2018 to @AOC—a rare and coveted three-letter moniker that reflected her growing influence. By the time she took the oath of office, Ocasio-Cortez had a larger audience on social media than the sixty other newly elected House Democrats combined, and larger even than the most powerful Democrat in the House, Speaker Nancy Pelosi. Although her number of Twitter followers amounted to a fraction of Donald Trump's 61 million, Ocasio-Cortez compared favorably to the president and other political leaders in terms of engagement. The freshman congresswoman boasted an interaction rate (the number of reactions, comments, and shares generated by an average post, divided by the total number of account followers) of 2.8 percent—or 28 engagements per 1,000 followers—compared to 0.2 percent for Trump and 0.4 percent for former president Barack Obama. Ocasio-Cortez's interaction rate translated to 17.5 million responses to her tweets in January 2019 alone, showing that many of her posts went viral online (Benwell 2019).

To some observers, Ocasio-Cortez stood at the forefront of a new generation of elected officials who brought American politics into the digital age. "Supporters and rivals alike agree that she has upended the traditional rules of engagement on Capitol Hill with a millennial's intuitive sense of what sells online," Shane Goldmacher wrote in *The New York Times* (Goldmacher 2019). With millennials (individuals born roughly between 1981 and 1996) predicted to overtake baby boomers (those born between 1946 and 1964) as the largest segment of the U.S. population in 2019—and 85 percent of millennials describing themselves as regular social media users—mastery of Twitter and other platforms promised to play an even more significant role for politicians in the future. "Politics is increasingly an exercise in digital marketing and creating content that has to compete for eyeballs with everyone from teenage influencers to major news outlets," said Alex Seitz-Wald of NBC News (Seitz-Wald 2019).

CONNECTING WITH PEOPLE

During her Democratic primary campaign against ten-term incumbent Joseph Crowley, Ocasio-Cortez used social media to build name recognition, spread her message, organize events, and mobilize volunteers. As a relatively unknown candidate, she gained exposure through social media that she never would have received from the traditional news media. Ocasio-Cortez used various platforms as a form of virtual canvassing to communicate directly with community members and establish personal relationships with potential supporters.

A key element of Ocasio-Cortez's social media campaign involved "The Courage to Change," the two-minute video she released a month before election day. It followed the candidate through her Bronx neighborhood—from her modest apartment to a local bodega and a nearby subway platform—as she described her working-class background and commitment to serving the community in a voiceover narrative. The viral video, which eventually received more than four million views, established a clear contrast between Ocasio-Cortez and her opponent. "She comes across as a very earnest, passionate person, not as a politician or a brand," Friedman stated. "This compares to Crowley, who comes across very much as establishment, with a neutral, bland voice, befitting the decorum of a Congressman" (Friedman 2018).

Ocasio-Cortez's authentic persona on social media helped voters identify with her, whereas Crowley's more generic persona made the career politician seem distant, disconnected, and out of touch (Friedman 2018). Some analysts attributed Ocasio-Cortez's upset victory to her superior social media presence, which appealed to the voters most likely to support her candidacy. "By virtue of her identity, her message, and her online medium, Ocasio-Cortez is speaking directly to young people, immigrants, and people of color, the nontraditional voters Democrats must energize," wrote Eliza Relman of *Insider*. "She won 80 percent of the votes cast in precincts in which the average voter was under 40" (Relman 2019).

Ocasio-Cortez continued using social media to connect with constituents—as well as a growing legion of fans across the country—after the election. The new congresswoman used Instagram stories and livestreams to document her thoughts and feelings as she prepared to take office, giving viewers an inside look at previously hidden aspects of the political process. Ocasio-Cortez filmed herself touring the library of Congress, admiring a portrait of Representative Shirley Chisholm (1924–2005), exploring the tunnels beneath the U.S. Capitol, joining a climate change protest outside Speaker Pelosi's office, and participating in the office lottery for members of Congress. Many observers appreciated how these posts made the workings of government more transparent and accessible for ordinary people. "Ocasio-Cortez uses Instagram like the rest of us do—reflexively, incidentally, the way you would if you were inside the United States Capitol at night, commenting on stuff in front of you," said Katherine Miller of BuzzFeed News. "She's acting like a regular person. She embodies this surrealist thing of, like, 'WHAT IF . . . *you were elected to Congress?* What would happen next? What would you do?'" (Miller 2018).

Ocasio-Cortez also used Instagram Live to explain her positions on important issues by speaking directly to the camera in an intimate, personal setting. She streamed one episode from her kitchen, answering questions from viewers as she listened to music and made macaroni and cheese. In other episodes, the congresswoman chatted candidly about her experiences and policy goals while assembling IKEA furniture in her living room and while potting plants in a community garden. "Ocasio-Cortez lives and breathes within Twitter and especially Instagram, and fluidly reacts to whatever is happening around her and whatever it is you're saying about her," Miller wrote. "Here's someone native to the way we use phones integrating politics into that, rather than the other way around. And it's fun. It's interesting. It's a good time" (Miller 2018).

Ocasio-Cortez hoped that her openness would encourage more regular, everyday Americans to run for political office. "I keep things raw and honest on here since I believe public servants do a disservice to our communities by pretending to be perfect," she posted on Instagram. "It makes things harder for others who aspire to run someday if they think they have to be superhuman before they even try" (Ocasio-Cortez 2018). Her post received more than a quarter-million "likes." One follower who appreciated the sentiment, Massachusetts resident Ashley Sorrondeguy, noted that "I always thought that in order to be a politician you needed inside connections or lots of money. It's really cool to see her in a real light" (Gonzalez-Ramirez 2019).

DUNKING ON CRITICS

Another aspect of Ocasio-Cortez's social media strategy involved using Twitter to respond directly to criticism or inaccurate information put forth by political opponents. As soon as Ocasio-Cortez's surprise primary victory thrust her into the national spotlight, conservative media outlets and right-wing commentators began releasing stories and statements intended to embarrass or discredit her. Beyond merely disagreeing with her political perspectives, critics jumped on every misstatement and questioned the freshman congresswoman's background, intelligence, physical appearance, and even her fashion choices. In many cases, Ocasio-Cortez used Twitter to defend herself and to set the record straight. Her pithy responses often flipped the script on her political opponents and created viral moments online, leading one journalist to dub her "the queen of savage comebacks" (Ankel 2018).

Unlike politicians who ceded control of their Twitter accounts to communications professionals, Ocasio-Cortez always composed her own tweets. "It's funny because a lot of people don't think I do," she acknowledged. "I was sitting next to a public official here in New York and I had pulled up my Twitter feed and I was drafting a tweet, and she was, like, 'You write those?' And I was, like, 'Yeah'" (Relman 2019). Although Ocasio-Cortez said she asked staff members to review her tweets only "once in a blue moon," she admitted to writing far more tweets than she actually posted. "There are so many tweets that do not see the light of day—there are so many," she stated. "In my house we joke: We call it 'emptying the cart.' It's like when you go online shopping and then you're, like, 'Oh no, never mind,' and you leave the website" (Relman 2019).

Most of Ocasio-Cortez's tweets offered her perspective on issues and events in the news. She also provided explanatory threads about her policy ideas, such as raising marginal tax rates on incomes over $10 million, expanding the federal Medicare program to provide affordable health care to all Americans, or improving the response to Hurricane Maria in Puerto Rico. Many of her viral tweets, however, featured clapbacks aimed at critics. Journalist Ta-Nehisi Coates asked Ocasio-Cortez how she decided whether to "dunk on fools" via Twitter. "Whoever is coming at me in my mentions with a blue check [indicating a public figure's verified account] when I haven't eaten in three hours," she responded. "And until more people start pitching in and holding people to account, I'm just going to let them have it" (Benwell 2019).

In August 2018, for instance, right-wing pundit Ben Shapiro challenged Ocasio-Cortez to a public debate, offering to donate $10,000 to a charity of her choice. She rejected his offer and called it sexist in a viral tweet. "Just like catcalling, I don't owe a response to unsolicited requests from men with bad intentions," she wrote. "And also like catcalling, for some reason they feel entitled to one" (Watling 2019). In December 2018, Ocasio-Cortez squared off against Donald Trump Jr. after the president's son posted a meme suggesting that adopting socialist policies would force Americans to eat their dogs. "It's funny cuz it's true!!!" he wrote. Ocasio-Cortez responded on Twitter by pointing out that the incoming Democrat-controlled House would soon gain the authority to investigate the Trump family's finances. "Please, keep it coming Jr—it's definitely a 'very, very large brain' idea to troll a member of a body that will have subpoena power in a month," she wrote (Mahdawi 2019). In January 2019, when House members voted for leadership roles, Ocasio-Cortez chastised her Republican colleagues in another tweet that went viral. "Over 200 members voted for Nancy Pelosi today, yet the GOP only booed one: me," she wrote. "Don't hate me cause you ain't me, fellas" (Goldmacher 2019).

Ocasio-Cortez also used Twitter to call out the conservative news organization Fox News for its intense scrutiny of her, which the liberal watchdog group Media Matters for America described as an "obsession." Fox News mentioned the first-term legislator dozens of times per day during her first few months in office, using her as "someone for hosts and guests to demonize, knock down, and refer to whenever grievances need to be aired against the Democratic Party" (Associated Press 2019). On several occasions, Ocasio-Cortez tweeted screenshots of graphics that the network used to generate outrage among its conservative viewers and changed the narrative by praising their accuracy. When Fox News aired a graphic titled "Radical New Democratic Ideas"—which included a list of such progressive priorities as free college tuition, free health care, and immediate action on the climate crisis, accompanied by photographs of Ocasio-Cortez and fellow congresswomen Ilhan Omar, Rashida Tlaib, and Ayanna Pressley—Ocasio-Cortez responded by tweeting, "Oh no! They've discovered our vast conspiracy to take care of children and save the planet!" (Watling 2019).

CONTROLLING THE NARRATIVE

Through her use of social media tools to connect with people and deflect criticism, Ocasio-Cortez effectively controlled the narrative of her political career and pushed her progressive ideas to the forefront of the national debate. "She's become a dominant presence in American politics," Miller stated. "She argues in threads, dunks on semi-randos, and is ready to mock the attempted sick own, harvesting and redirecting its power" (Miller 2018). By virtue of her huge social media following, Ocasio-Cortez gained prominence in the traditional news media—and the media attention, in turn, generated additional followers for her social media accounts. "Tweets, dunks, and livestreams beget media appearances and coverage; the media appearances and coverage beget more tweets, dunks, and livestreams. The cycle repeats. And it works," Warzel wrote. "It's agenda-setting. Constant content creation forces your opponent to respond to *you*. It's a strategy that's working fantastically well for Ocasio-Cortez, who's pulled off the rare Trump-era feat of dominating online and cable news cycles virtually every day since she was sworn into office" (Warzel 2019).

Some observers compared Ocasio-Cortez's combative use of Twitter to President Trump's, noting that they both demonstrated an ability to shift political discussions and control the news cycle. "The ability to take your message and yourself directly to people is perhaps one of this era's most important talents. In this, as much as she'd hate to admit it, Ms. Ocasio-Cortez is following in the footsteps of President Trump," Kara Swisher wrote in *The New York Times*. "[But] while he spouts outward, turning into an online megaphone, Ms. Ocasio-Cortez listens, takes everything in and reacts. Both methods work. And she is the only one who can keep up with him online" (Swisher 2019).

Other political leaders—including several 2020 Democratic presidential candidates—tried to emulate Ocasio-Cortez's social media presence by allowing the public to see intimate details of their lives. Elizabeth Warren (D-MA) filmed herself opening a beer in her kitchen to announce her campaign, for instance, while Beto O'Rourke (D-TX) livestreamed himself undergoing a dental cleaning. Yet they struggled to appear as natural and open online as Ocasio-Cortez and a few of her millennial colleagues who grew up during the digital age. "People have exquisitely well-developed bulls—meters," warned Representative Jim Himes (D-CT). "Almost every real tweet is going to involve a little bit of risk. It's going to be a little bit of opening the kimono into a member's private life, because a little bit of risk is authentic" (Seitz-Wald 2019).

In January 2019, the House Democratic Policy and Communications Committee invited Ocasio-Cortez and Himes to give their Democratic colleagues a tutorial on social media usage. A notice sent out by committee members said the session covered "the importance of digital storytelling" and offered tips on how to "use Twitter as an effective and authentic messaging tool to connect with their constituents" (Serfaty and Sullivan 2019). "Class was in session this morning!" Ocasio-Cortez tweeted. "I was thrilled to offer some insights on Twitter and social media to my colleagues" (Serfaty and Sullivan 2019).

Afterward, Ocasio-Cortez appeared on *The Late Show with Stephen Colbert* and told the host about the advice she had given to House Democrats. "Rule number one is to be authentic, be yourself, and don't try to be anyone that you're not," she explained. "Don't try to talk like a young kid if you're not a young kid, don't post a meme if you don't know what a meme is—that was literally my advice—and I said don't talk like the Founding Fathers on Twitter. If you're a mom that likes to garden, talk like a mom that likes to garden, that's all you gotta do" (Watling 2019). "We were both trying to hammer home this message of, 'Speak like yourself, be a human,'" Himes added. "Anything you can do to close the gap between the blow-dried, poll-tested, bullet-pointed politician and the people" (Seitz-Wald 2019).

Even as Ocasio-Cortez gained a reputation as an expert in the use of social media tools to achieve political goals, she also recognized the potential pitfalls of excessive reliance on the technology. In April 2019, the congresswoman announced that she closed her personal account on Facebook, citing concerns about privacy and security on the platform as well as its negative impact on her well-being. Ocasio-Cortez praised the role Facebook played as a digital organizing tool for her campaign, however, and noted that her staff still maintained her official congressional Facebook account as well as an account dedicated to political advertising. Although Ocasio-Cortez continued to post prolifically on Twitter and Instagram, she also vowed to cut back on her consumption of social media content on weekends. "I actually think that social media poses a public health risk to everybody," she stated. "There are amplified impacts for young people, particularly children under the age of 3, with screen time, but I think it has a lot of effects on older people. I think it has effects on everybody: increased isolation, depression, anxiety, addiction, escapism" (Watkins 2019).

KNOCK DOWN THE HOUSE

In keeping with her openness on social media, Alexandria Ocasio-Cortez agreed to give a documentary film crew intimate, behind-the-scenes access to her primary election campaign. Filmmaker Rachel Lears recognized that disappointment and anger over the results of the 2016 presidential election had inspired a record number of women to run for office in the 2018 midterms. Her documentary *Knock Down the House* chronicles the campaigns of four progressive, working-class women who attempt to unseat established Democratic incumbents with the backing of Justice Democrats and Brand New Congress. In addition to Ocasio-Cortez in New York, the movie follows Cori Bush, an African American nurse who became politically active during the racial violence in Ferguson, Missouri; Paula Jean Swearengin, a coal miner's daughter galvanized by environmental destruction and high cancer rates in West Virginia; and Amy Vilela, a Nevada businesswoman who became a health care activist following her daughter's death from a treatable medical condition.

Knock Down the House shows the long hours and hard work involved in running a grassroots, insurgent campaign. The film captures Ocasio-Cortez working as a bartender, canvassing door to door in her Bronx neighborhood, getting her signatures certified by the election board, giving herself a pep talk in her apartment, debating against her opponent, and realizing that she won the election. "I'm just so glad that this moment for the four of us was captured and documented," Ocasio-Cortez said. "Not just for the personal meaning of it, but for everyday people to see that yes, this is incredibly challenging and yes, the odds are long, but also yes, that it's worth it. Each and every person who submits themselves to run for office is doing a great service to this country" (Ryan 2019). Although Ocasio-Cortez was the only candidate profiled who won her primary, the film presents her underdog story within the context of the larger progressive movement. "It's just the reality that in order for one of us to make it through, a hundred of us have to try," she said in consoling Vilela (Lowry 2019).

Knock Down the House premiered at the Sundance Film Festival in January 2019. Ocasio-Cortez made a surprise appearance via videoconference and received a standing ovation from the audience. Netflix acquired distribution rights to the film and made it available for streaming in May 2019. "This here, right now, is an unstoppable movement, and this scattered yet succinct documentary bottles up its All-American can-do spirit," wrote reviewer Nick Allen. "Lears' stirring document is a worthwhile reminder for American citizens of the importance of making one's voice heard" (Allen 2019).

FURTHER READING

Allen, Nick. 2019. "*Knock Down the House.*" RogerEbert.com, May 1, 2019. https://www.rogerebert.com/reviews/knock-down-the-house-2019.

Ankel, Sophia. 2018. "Alexandria Ocasio-Cortez Just Trolled Fox News by Saying They're Obsessed with Her." *Independent*, November 25, 2018. https://www.indy100.com/article/alexandria-ocasio-cortez-fox-news-spanish-translation-tweet-democrat-twitter-8650721.

Associated Press. 2019. "Study: Fox News Is Obsessed with Alexandria Ocasio-Cortez." *USA Today*, April 14, 2019. https://www

.usatoday.com/story/life/tv/2019/04/14/study-fox-news-obsessed-alexandria-ocasio-cortez/3466493002/.

Benwell, Max. 2019. "How Alexandria Ocasio-Cortez Beat Everyone at Twitter in Nine Tweets." *Guardian*, February 12, 2019. https://www.theguardian.com/us-news/2019/feb/12/alexandria-ocasio-cortez-twitter-social-media.

Dale, Frank. 2018. "Alexandria Ocasio-Cortez Is Changing the Way Politicians Use Social Media." ThinkProgress, December 4, 2018. https://thinkprogress.org/alexandria-ocasio-cortez-social-media-house-democrats-twitter-instagram-stories-democratic-socialist-congress-01a76857a3d2/.

Dwyer, Devin. 2019. "Alexandria Ocasio-Cortez's Twitter Lesson for House Democrats." NBC News, January 17, 2019. https://abc news.go.com/beta-story-container/Politics/alexandria-ocasio-cor tezs-twitter-lesson-house-democrats/story?id=60443727.

Friedman, Peter. 2018. "The 2018 Social Media Political Wars: How Alexandria Ocasio-Cortez Used Social Media to Beat Joe Crowley." LiveWorld, July 6, 2018. https://www.liveworld .com/2018-social-media-political-wars-how-ocasio-cortez-used-social-media-beat-joe-crowley/.

Goldmacher, Shane. 2019. "Ocasio-Cortez Pushes Democrats to the Left, whether They Like It or Not." *The New York Times*, January 13, 2019. https://www.nytimes.com/2019/01/13/nyregion/ocasio-cortez-democrats-congress.html.

Gonzalez-Ramirez, Andrea. 2019. "How Alexandria Ocasio-Cortez's Obsession-Worthy Instagram Is Changing the Game." Refinery 29, April 17, 2019. https://www.refinery29.com/en-us/2019/04/229351/alexandria-ocasio-cortez-instagram-live-social-media-message.

Lowry, Brian. 2019. "*Knock Down the House* Puts AOC's Stunning Victory in Larger Context." CNN, April 30, 2019. https://www .cnn.com/2019/04/30/entertainment/knock-down-the-house-review/index.html.

Mahdawi, Arwa. 2019. "Ocasio-Cortez Outrages Republicans by Refusing to Respect Their Ignorance." *Guardian*, March 2, 2019. https://www.theguardian.com/world/2019/mar/02/alexan dria-ocasio-cortez-republicans-ignorance.

Miller, Katherine. 2018. "Why Alexandria Ocasio-Cortez's Instagram Is So Good." BuzzFeed News, November 21, 2018.
https://www.buzzfeednews.com/article/katherinemiller/alexa
ndria-ocasio-cortez-instagram.

Minsberg, Talya. 2018. "How Alexandria Ocasio-Cortez Is Bringing Her Instagram Followers into the Political Process." *The
New York Times*, November 16, 2018. https://www.nytimes
.com/2018/11/16/us/politics/ocasio-cortez-instagram-congress
.html.

Ocasio-Cortez, Alexandria. 2018. Instagram, Ocasio2018, December 29, 2018. https://www.instagram.com/p/Br-jt_IBWJk/.

Relman, Eliza. 2019. "The Truth about Alexandria Ocasio-Cortez."
Insider, January 6, 2019. https://www.thisisinsider.com/alexand
ria-ocasio-cortez-biography-2019-1.

Ryan, Patrick. 2019. "Alexandria Ocasio-Cortez Surprises at Premiere
of Her Emotional New Documentary." *USA Today*, January 28,
2019.   https://www.usatoday.com/story/life/movies/2019/01/27/
alexandria-ocasio-cortez-surprises-sundance-premiere-her-new-
doc/2698284002/.

Seitz-Wald, Alex. 2019. "Democrats 'Like' It: The Secret to Ocasio-
Cortez's Social Media Success." NBC News, January 20, 2019.
https://www.nbcnews.com/politics/2020-election/democrats-it-
secret-ocasio-cortez-s-social-media-success-n960561.

Serfaty, Sunlen, and Kate Sullivan. 2019. "Alexandria Ocasio-Cortez Gave Her Democratic Colleagues Twitter Training." CNN,
January 17, 2019. https://www.cnn.com/2019/01/16/politics/aoc-
twitter-congress/index.html.

Swisher, Kara. 2019. "Trump vs. Ocasio-Cortez: Who Will Win the
Internet?" *The New York Times*, January 10, 2019. https://www
.nytimes.com/2019/01/10/opinion/ocasio-cortez-aoc-trump.html.

Warzel, Charlie. 2019. "Alexandria Ocasio-Cortez Is a Perfect Foil
for the Pro-Trump Media." BuzzFeed News, January 7, 2019.
https://www.buzzfeednews.com/article/charliewarzel/alexa
ndria-ocasio-cortez-is-a-perfect-foil-for-the-pro.

Watkins, Eli. 2019. "Social Media Titan Ocasio-Cortez Warns about
'Public Health Risk' from Online Platforms." CNN, April 15,

2019. https://www.cnn.com/2019/04/15/politics/alexandria-oca sio-cortez-social-media/index.html.

Watling, Eve. 2019. "Alexandria Ocasio-Cortez Twitter Timeline: Tracking AOC's Transformation into a Twitter Giant, One Tweet at a Time." *Newsweek*, January 24, 2019. https://www.newsweek .com/alexandria-ocasio-cortez-twitter-social-media-1303609.

Chapter 11

ISSUES AND POSITIONS

Justice is not a concept we read about in a book. Justice is about the water we drink. Justice is about the air we breathe. Justice is about how easy is it to vote. Justice is about how much ladies get paid. Justice is about making sure that being polite is not the same thing as being quiet. In fact, oftentimes, the most righteous thing you can do is shake the table. (McDonald 2019)

Alexandria Ocasio-Cortez ran for Congress in 2018 on a platform of unapologetically progressive ideas. Her primary opponent, Joseph Crowley, rose through the ranks of the Democratic Party by reliably voting to support moderate-to-liberal party priorities during his two decades in office. Yet Ocasio-Cortez challenged him from the left with a grassroots, insurgent campaign that portrayed Crowley as a career politician beholden to big-money special interests and out of touch with his constituents. When the democratic socialist newcomer unseated the ten-term incumbent, many political analysts placed her victory within the context of the larger progressive movement that arose in opposition to the election of Donald Trump. They predicted that Ocasio-Cortez—as a young, progressive woman of color—would serve as a face of this movement and help shift the overall Democratic Party leftward.

As she prepared to take office, the freshman congresswoman emphasized her belief that Democrats needed to pursue bold policy goals that went beyond resisting the Trump administration and presented a compelling future direction for the country. "We have to stick to the message: What are we proposing to the American people? Not, 'What are we fighting against?'" she stated. "We understand that we're under an antagonistic administration, but what is the vision that is going to earn and deserve the support of working-class Americans? And we need to be explicit in that vision and legislation, not just 'better,' but what exactly is our plan?" (Clark 2018). Both during her campaign and during her first months in office, Ocasio-Cortez outlined her positions on the major issues she felt Congress should address. The first piece of legislation she introduced, House Resolution 109, combined many of her progressive priorities in the Green New Deal, a wide-ranging plan to combat global climate change and stimulate the U.S. economy by transitioning to 100 percent clean and renewable energy sources.

PROMOTING PROGRESSIVE IDEAS

Taking a plank from Senator Bernie Sanders's 2016 presidential campaign platform, Ocasio-Cortez expressed support for Medicare for All—a proposal to expand the federal Medicare program to give all Americans access to government-run health care. Ocasio-Cortez described high-quality, affordable medical services as a fundamental human right that millions of Americans lacked due to the high cost and limited coverage provided by private, for-profit health insurance companies. "Almost every other developed nation in the world has universal healthcare," she said on her campaign website. "It's time the United States catch up to the rest of the world in ensuring all people have real healthcare coverage that doesn't break the bank" (Ocasio-Cortez 2018). Ocasio-Cortez argued that converting to a single-payer health care system financed by federal tax revenues would reduce costs, increase benefits, and ensure coverage for more Americans.

Critics of the Medicare for All proposal, on the other hand, claimed that competition in a free-market health insurance system was the best way to preserve consumer choice and medical innovation. They also asserted that doing away with private insurance would cause painful disruptions in hospital services and other areas of the health care industry. According to Ocasio-Cortez, large hospital systems and pharmaceutical companies promoted this opposing view in order to protect their financial interests.

Ocasio-Cortez also expressed support for a number of progressive policy proposals intended to raise the standard of living for working-class Americans and address the problem of growing economic inequality. For example, she endorsed a federal jobs guarantee for "anyone who is willing and able to work," according to her campaign website. Under this plan, Americans who were unable to find employment in the private sector would receive government jobs that offered a $15 minimum wage and basic benefits, including health care, child care, and paid sick leave. "This proposal would dramatically upgrade the quality of employment in the United States," Ocasio-Cortez said on her website, "by providing training and experience to workers while bringing much-needed public services to our communities in areas such as parks service, child care, and environmental conservation" (Ocasio-Cortez 2018). She also argued that the federal jobs guarantee would shift power from corporations back to workers and lift families out of poverty.

Ivanka Trump, the president's daughter and a senior White House adviser, criticized the proposal. She claimed that American workers were prospering under the administration's economic programs and did not want what she described as a free handout. "I don't think most Americans, in their heart, want to be given something," Trump said. "People want to work for what they get. So, I think that this idea of a guaranteed minimum is not something most people want. They want the ability to be able to secure a job. They want the ability to live in a country where's there's the potential for upward mobility" (Garcia 2019). Ocasio-Cortez responded with one of her famous Twitter clapbacks. "As a person who actually worked for tips and hourly wages in my life, instead of having to learn about it secondhand, I can tell you that most people want to be paid enough to live," she tweeted. "A living wage isn't a gift, it's a right. Workers are often paid far less than the value they create" (Garcia 2019).

Ocasio-Cortez also described affordable housing as a basic right that was no longer available to many Americans—especially in her district—due to real estate speculation and gentrification of working-class neighborhoods. "Housing in the United States has become a playground for wealthy developers instead of a leg up towards the American Dream," she stated on her website. "In New York City specifically, money from luxury real estate developers has taken over our political establishment—leading to luxury rezonings that push out small businesses and working families, and leave a wake of empty units in their place" (Ocasio-Cortez 2018). The congresswoman noted that her mother, after years of fighting to keep the family home, finally moved to Florida during the campaign to escape skyrocketing property-tax rates in New York. "I was paying $10,000 a year in real estate taxes up north," Blanca explained. "I'm paying $600 a year in Florida. It's stress-free down here" (Lambiet 2019). Ocasio-Cortez supported fair housing policies designed to help working families and middle-class homeowners, including tax credits and investments in affordable housing development.

Like several other progressive Democrats, Ocasio-Cortez sought to address the effects of economic inequality, create a highly trained workforce, and lift families out of poverty by offering tuition-free public college. "Roughly every 100 years, the United States expands its public education system to match its increasingly advanced economy," she said on her website. "It's now time to expand our national education system to include tuition-free public college and trade school" (Ocasio-Cortez 2018). She pointed out that the City University of New York, the University of California system, and many other institutions had not started charging tuition until the late twentieth century. By 2018, however, rapidly rising tuition rates had put higher education out of reach for many low-income students.

As someone who struggled for years to pay off student loans, Ocasio-Cortez also supported federal student-debt forgiveness, which she claimed would enable millennials to purchase homes and cars and otherwise participate in the U.S. economy. "For the cost of the GOP tax cut that was passed in 2017, we could have forgiven every single student loan," she told a group of students at John Jay College in New York. "So the question is not about possibility; it's a question of priority.

And what [the Republicans] told us is that a handful of billionaires are more important than educating our entire populace at the level that our economy demands" (Gressier 2019).

Ocasio-Cortez's platform also featured planks promoting progressive policies on criminal justice reform and gun control. She called for new legislation to prevent gun violence, such as reinstating the federal ban on assault weapons, banning high-capacity magazines and bump stocks, mandating universal background checks for all gun purchases, and requiring domestic abusers to surrender their firearms. In addition, Ocasio-Cortez suggested prohibiting members of Congress from accepting campaign donations from the firearms industry. "Instead of fighting to save American lives, politicians bend over backwards to protect the billionaire-backed gun lobby," she declared on her website. "Gun lobby money is the number one barrier to getting any meaningful action on guns accomplished in Congress. The NRA has invested millions of dollars to make sure our politicians keep our gun laws weak and our children at risk" (Ocasio-Cortez 2018).

In the area of criminal justice reform, Ocasio-Cortez promoted policies aimed at ending mass incarceration, which she described as "the latest iteration of a long line of policies (Jim Crow, redlining, etc.) rooted in the marginalization of African Americans and people of color" (Ocasio-Cortez 2018). She proposed releasing people incarcerated for nonviolent drug offenses and legalizing marijuana. She also suggested abolishing cash bail, ending for-profit prisons, demilitarizing police departments, and requiring independent investigations whenever civilians were killed by law enforcement. Ocasio-Cortez contended that decades of "tough on crime" policies had created an unfair system that needed a complete overhaul. "Our country has a 'justice' system that criminalizes poverty [and] disproportionately targets race, yet routinely pardons large-scale crimes of wealth and privilege," she tweeted. "It's less a justice system, and more a class enforcement system" (Da Silva 2019).

Ocasio-Cortez generally followed the Democratic Party line by expressing strong support for women's rights. On her campaign website, she promised to fight to ensure that all working women enjoyed equal pay, paid parental leave, and full access to health care, including "safe, legal, affordable abortion, birth control, and family planning services, as well as access to adequate, affordable pre- and post-natal care" (Ocasio-Cortez 2018). Ocasio-Cortez also declared her solidarity with the LGBTQIA+ community and promised to fight against discriminatory Trump administration policies "that would deny many people their rights to basic employment, housing, healthcare, and education on the basis of gender identity and sexual orientation." She also noted that "the issues facing the LGBTQIA+ community are not isolated from the issues facing many of us regarding race and class. It is critical in times like these that we stand together in solidarity, to build just public policy that works for all of us, not just some of us" (Ocasio-Cortez 2018).

According to Ocasio-Cortez, campaign finance reform provided the key to meaningful government reform. She asserted that the 2010 U.S. Supreme Court ruling in *Citizens United v. Federal Election Commission* gave wealthy individuals, corporations, and political action committees the ability to purchase influence at all levels of government "with unaccountable dark money." She called for legislation to overturn the decision, reform campaign finance laws to require full disclosure of political contributions, and establish public funding of elections. Recognizing the potential for lobbyist contributions to corrupt the legislative process, Ocasio-Cortez also refused to accept any campaign funding from corporate interests. "This is not a progressive or a conservative issue," she said. "It is an issue that should concern all Americans, regardless of their political point of view, who wish to preserve the longest-standing democracy in the world, and a government that represents all of the people and not a handful of powerful and wealthy special interests" (Ocasio-Cortez 2018).

Political opponents and conservative media outlets derided Ocasio-Cortez's progressive platform as radical, dangerous, and a threat to American democracy. Many critics claimed that she sought to overthrow capitalism and install a socialist system of government. "I worry as an American about the direction of one of our two major parties going toward socialist," said former House Majority Leader Eric Cantor (R-VA). "I've heard a new acronym, a new meaning for that acronym [AOC]: 'absolutely out of control,' if you think about what she's putting out there" (Belvedere 2019).

Supporters, on the other hand, argued that Ocasio-Cortez's platform marked a return to earlier eras of progressive politics, when government played an active role in improving citizens' lives and ensuring that everyone benefited from the nation's prosperity. They attributed the intense opposition she encountered to extreme partisan politics. When conservative pundit Sean Hannity condemned Ocasio-Cortez on Fox News, for instance, the screen behind him showed a graphic listing the main points in the incoming congresswoman's platform. "Except they failed to run the graphic through the normally rigorous process of Fox News scaremongerization and white-resentment optimization. They just put it up there, spin-free, and it looked . . . pretty reasonable," Jack Holmes wrote in *Esquire*. "More than just discounting these policy prescriptions, though, Hannity's tone communicates that he finds the very *idea* we'd be interested in every American having housing to be absurd. He does not even acknowledge this as a possible goal of society. . . . That would mean The Losers getting something They Don't Deserve. And that is the cancer at the root of the Fox News resentment machine" (Holmes 2018).

REFORMING IMMIGRATION LAWS

During her campaign to represent one of the most diverse districts in the nation, Ocasio-Cortez ran on a platform advocating "immigration justice." One plank of this platform called for legislation providing permanent legal status for participants in the Deferred Action for Childhood Arrivals (DACA) program, which offered temporary, renewable protection from deportation for approximately 700,000 undocumented immigrants who arrived in the United States as children. DACA supporters pointed out that most of these individuals had grown up as Americans and had little connection to their countries of origin. DACA gave them access to education and work permits, which enabled them to become productive members of American society. The Trump administration sought to end the program. Critics argued that President Barack Obama had exceeded his authority by establishing DACA via executive order, and they further claimed that the program took jobs from native-born Americans and encouraged unaccompanied minors to enter the United States illegally.

Ocasio-Cortez also supported legislation to establish a clear path to citizenship for undocumented immigrants residing in the United

States. She said her employment in the food-service industry, where undocumented people fill around one-third of all jobs nationwide (Cadigan 2018), gave her a deeper, more personal understanding of the political issues surrounding immigration. By working alongside both documented and undocumented immigrants, Ocasio-Cortez learned how the threat of raids, arrests, and deportations by U.S. Immigration and Customs Enforcement (ICE) agents created fear and uncertainty in people's lives. At a busy Manhattan diner called The Coffee Shop, for instance, she worked with a brunch chef known as "Grande" who "ran the line like clockwork" for fifteen years. Following the election of Trump, however, the growing threat of ICE raids convinced Grande to quit and return to Mexico. The restaurant struggled so much in his absence that it ended up closing. "You can't hire that back. That stuff takes years to perfect," Ocasio-Cortez explained. "Our kitchen got all messed up. We had to change our brunch menu because we couldn't handle the same volume of orders anymore" (Cadigan 2018).

The Trump administration stepped up enforcement of existing immigration laws, banned immigration from certain Muslim-majority countries in the Middle East, established new limits on refugee admissions, and promised to construct a wall along the 1,900-mile U.S.-Mexico border. The Trump administration also empowered ICE to round up and deport undocumented immigrants. During Trump's first one hundred days in office in 2017, ICE arrests increased by 38 percent over the previous year (Cadigan 2018). Whereas ICE had previously focused on deporting immigrants with criminal records, the agency instead began launching highly visible raids on communities and industries with large immigrant populations. Supporters of this policy change argued that all undocumented immigrants broke the law by entering the country illegally. They portrayed immigrants as a drain on the nation's resources and claimed that strict enforcement by ICE would encourage other aliens to "self-deport," or leave of their own accord.

Opponents, on the other hand, described ICE tactics as indiscriminate and brutal. They asserted that the agency operated above the law to harass and terrorize productive, law-abiding people—some of whom had lived, worked, and raised families in the United States for many years. They characterized Trump's immigration policies as rooted in racist and white-supremacist views and as a violation of fundamental human rights. Ocasio-Cortez emerged as a vocal critic of ICE and a leading advocate of abolishing the agency. "As overseen by the Trump administration, ICE operates with virtually no accountability, ripping apart families and holding our friends and neighbors indefinitely in inhumane detention centers scattered across the United States," she stated on her website (Ocasio-Cortez 2018).

Ocasio-Cortez pointed out that ICE had been established in response to the terrorist attacks against the United States of September 11, 2001, as part of the Department of Homeland Security. As a result, she contended, ICE agents viewed immigrants and people of color with suspicion and treated them as potential threats to national security. "There were many Democrats who voted against the creation of ICE at its inception in 2003," she noted.

> We knew back then, in the post–9/11 push of authoritarian legislation—the Patriot Act, the authorization of the Iraq War—that the systems that were being established in this time were extrajudicial. They do not meet the tests of our Constitutional right to due process in the United States. . . . For a very long time, ICE has had a documented history of sexual assault, of unaccountable deaths, of unethical practices happening in their facilities. What we need to realize is that the Trump administration is taking an already unjust structure and pushing it to its most extreme. But that unjust structure has been there from the very beginning. (Paiella 2018)

Ocasio-Cortez sought to abolish ICE, launch a congressional inquiry into the agency's practices, and help individuals and communities harmed by ICE misconduct.

When Ocasio-Cortez and other members of the 116th Congress took office in January 2019, the federal government was mired in what became the longest shutdown in its history, mainly due to a disagreement between President Trump and Congress over immigration policy. Trump demanded $5.7 billion to construct a wall along the southern border of the United States, arguing that a physical barrier was needed to prevent immigrants from Mexico and Central America from entering the country illegally. He claimed that "migrant caravans" overwhelmed border security and brought drugs, weapons, crime, and gang violence with them to the United States. Democrats denied funding for the wall, calling it impractical and unnecessary, and characterized the migrants as families seeking asylum in the United States after fleeing political instability, persecution, and violence in their countries of origin. The standoff finally ended on January 25, when Trump signed a spending bill to reopen the government that did not allocate money for his border wall.

Ocasio-Cortez opposed border-wall funding as well as Trump administration policies that involved detaining asylum seekers at the border. In June 2018, just a few days before her primary election, she flew to El Paso, Texas, to participate in a protest against Trump's "zero-tolerance" policy. Under this policy, migrant families were being separated at the border, with children detained apart from their parents as the adults awaited prosecution and deportation. A year later, the congresswoman joined a group of fourteen Democratic lawmakers from the Congressional Hispanic Caucus on a tour of two immigrant-detention facilities in Texas. Several members of the group reported that detainees—including unaccompanied minors—were being held in terrible, unsanitary conditions. Ocasio-Cortez, who spoke to some of the detainees, tweeted that they had not been allowed to shower for more than two weeks, had been forced to drink out of toilets, and had been subjected to psychological abuse by guards. Other observers reported extreme overcrowding, with hundreds of migrants being held in chain-link enclosures, sleeping on concrete floors, wearing filthy clothing, and being denied access to basic necessities and medical care.

Trump and other administration officials denied that migrants were being held in cruel or inhumane conditions. "I've seen some of those places and they are run beautifully," Trump stated. "They're clean. They are good. They do a great job" (Warikoo 2019). The president also responded to reports of poor treatment by pointing out that migrants broke the law by entering the United States illegally. "If illegal immigrants are unhappy with the conditions in the quickly built or refitted detention centers, just tell them not to come. All problems solved!" Trump tweeted (Warikoo 2019). Some Trump supporters tried to shift attention away from detention-camp conditions by attacking the critics who raised questions about them. Following Ocasio-Cortez's visit, conservative news outlets claimed that she had "screamed at" and threatened guards at the detention facilities and refused to follow the designated tour schedule. Although the congresswoman denied the reports, her supporters argued that the situation warranted an angry response. "The entire news cycle surrounding the congresswoman's behavior was an example of how debates about political violence get subsumed by debates about civility," Zak Cheney-Rice wrote in *New York Magazine*. "Ocasio-Cortez is now compelled to defend behavior that, had she even engaged in it, would have been reasonable given the circumstances. Instead, it is being used to illustrate her unreasonability relative to those who incarcerate and functionally torture people for not having immigration papers" (Cheney-Rice 2019).

Ocasio-Cortez also generated controversy by declaring on Instagram that "the United States is running concentration camps on our southern border" (Beinert 2019). Conservative critics objected to her choice of terminology, asserting that it unfairly equated Trump's migrant-detention policies with the Nazi genocide that resulted in the extermination of six million Jews during the Holocaust. Once again, the congresswoman's supporters argued that Republicans preferred to debate about semantics rather than address the humanitarian crisis at the border. "Whatever the merits of her criticism, when those in power are caught abusing that power in ways that are morally indefensible and politically unpopular, they will always seek to turn an argument about oppression into a dispute about manners," Adam Serwer wrote in the *Atlantic*. "If congressional Republicans—or, for that matter, their constituents—had expressed a fraction as much outrage over the treatment of migrant children in American detention facilities as they did in response to Ocasio-Cortez's remarks, she would never have had cause to make them in the first place" (Serwer 2019).

PROPOSING A GREEN NEW DEAL

Ocasio-Cortez also campaigned on a platform that demanded bold, aggressive action to combat global climate change. "Climate change is the single biggest national security threat for the United States and the single biggest threat to worldwide industrialized civilization, and the effects of warming can be hard to predict and self-reinforcing," she noted on her website. "We need to avoid a worldwide refugee crisis by waging a war for climate justice through the mobilization of our population and our government. This starts with the United States being a leader on the actions we take both globally and locally" (Ocasio-Cortez 2018). In December 2018, during the orientation period for new members of Congress, Ocasio-Cortez joined a Sunrise Movement climate-change demonstration outside the office of fellow Democrat Nancy Pelosi (D-CA). Pointing to a United Nations report warning that irrevocable changes would occur within twelve years if world leaders failed to address the problem immediately, the protesters called on the presumptive House speaker to create a select committee dedicated to developing a detailed U.S. climate-change action plan.

After taking office, Ocasio-Cortez made climate change the focus of the first piece of legislation she sponsored. On February 7, 2019, she introduced HR 109, "Recognizing the Duty of the Federal Government to Create a Green New Deal," while Senator Ed Markey (D-MA) submitted a joint resolution in the Senate as SR 59. The Green New Deal took its name from the New Deal economic stimulus and social reform measures implemented by President Franklin D. Roosevelt to relieve poverty, create jobs, and restore prosperity during the Great Depression of the 1930s. The new proposal established a similarly ambitious framework for mobilizing the nation's resources to combat climate change and address economic inequality. "Even the solutions that we have considered big and bold are nowhere near the scale of the actual problem that climate change presents to us," Ocasio-Cortez stated (Kurtzleben 2019). "It's time to shift course and implement a Green New Deal—a transformation that implements structural changes to our political and financial systems in order to alter the trajectory of our environment. . . . The Green New Deal believes that radically addressing climate change is a potential path towards a more equitable economy with increased employment and widespread financial security for all" (Ocasio-Cortez 2018).

The fourteen-page, nonbinding resolution laid out a plan to transition the United States to 100 percent clean and renewable energy by 2035. It called for phasing out fossil fuel extraction, overhauling power generation and transportation to eliminate greenhouse gas emissions, remodeling buildings and infrastructure to emphasize energy efficiency, and working with industry and agriculture to achieve sustainable production. In addition to such measures aimed at curbing the effects of climate change, the Green New Deal also incorporated a number of progressive social reform policies intended to create a more fair and just economy, such as a federal jobs guarantee, a minimum wage increase, universal health care, affordable housing, and tuition-free public college. The stated goals of HR 19 included the following:

(A) to achieve net-zero greenhouse gas emissions through a fair and just transition for all communities and workers;

(B) to create millions of good, high-wage jobs and ensure prosperity and economic security for all people of the United States;

(C) to invest in the infrastructure and industry of the United States to sustainably meet the challenges of the 21st century;

(D) to secure for all people of the United States for generations to come—
   (i) clean air and water;
   (ii) climate and community resiliency;
   (iii) healthy food;
   (iv) access to nature; and
   (v) a sustainable environment; and

(E) to promote justice and equity by stopping current, preventing future, and repairing historic oppression of indigenous peoples, communities of color, migrant communities, deindustrialized communities, depopulated rural communities, the poor, low-income workers, women, the elderly, the unhoused, people with disabilities, and youth. (116th Congress 2019)

According to Ocasio-Cortez and other Green New Deal proponents, climate change grew out of a capitalist system in which powerful corporations maximized profits at the expense of workers and the environment. In addition, the impacts of climate change, pollution, and environmental degradation disproportionately harmed poor and minority communities, which exacerbated economic injustice. To combat climate change, therefore, also meant changing the system to eliminate economic inequality. "[The Green New Deal's] intent is to involve the entire citizenry in the shared project of adapting to the

21st century, and in so doing materially improve the quality of life of the poor and middle class," explained David Roberts of Vox. "It is an attempt to rebalance the economy and the political system, away from a monomaniacal focus on private goods, toward a more generous view of public goods and public purpose" (Roberts 2019a).

As the most visible proponent of the Green New Deal, Ocasio-Cortez helped generate national attention for her plan to address the climate crisis. More than 600 organizations representing millions of members sent a letter to Congress demanding "visionary and affirmative legislative action" to address the "urgent threat" posed by climate change. The signees included Friends of the Earth, Greenpeace, Sierra Club, and the Sunrise Movement (Friends of the Earth 2019). The Green New Deal brought climate change to the forefront of policy debates heading into the 2020 presidential race. Most of the twenty candidates seeking the Democratic nomination either signed on as cosponsors of the legislation or expressed support for its goals, although a few requested more details or released climate-change plans of their own. Speaker Pelosi expressed reservations about the Green New Deal, however, and insisted that congressional Democrats would consider a variety of approaches to the climate crisis.

The Green New Deal received some criticism from political moderates and mainstream news outlets. Some detractors asserted that the proposal was overly broad and ambitious, which made it too complex for the public to understand and reduced its chances of being adopted. Ocasio-Cortez and other sponsors defended the scope of the Green New Deal by saying that the country needed a massive mobilization—on the scale of World War II or the Moon landing—to adequately prepare for the catastrophic effects of climate change. Other critics complained that the Green New Deal was too vague and lacked details. Ocasio-Cortez noted that she intended for the nonbinding resolution to provide a general framework or vision, with the details to be worked out through legislative debate and consultation with private-sector interests. Finally, many critics insisted that the proposal was too expensive and questioned how the nation would pay for it. Ocasio-Cortez and other supporters noted that the damaging effects of climate change would be even more costly if the United States failed to take action. They also pointed out that the government spent billions of dollars on tax cuts, defense spending, and other Republican priorities without worrying about the source of the funding. Finally, Ocasio-Cortez suggested several options to raise revenue to help pay for the Green New Deal, including a marginal tax rate of 70 percent on incomes over $10 million per year.

Republican leaders and conservative media outlets strongly opposed the Green New Deal, calling it a radical socialist program that would destroy the U.S. economy. Senator Tom Cotton (R-AR) warned that Ocasio-Cortez wanted to "confiscate every privately owned vehicle in America within a decade and ban air travel so we could all drive or ride around on high-speed light rail, supposedly powered by unicorn tears" (Schwartz 2019). Other critics claimed that Green New Deal proponents sought to ban livestock and prevent the American people from consuming milkshakes and hamburgers. "The proposal we are talking about is, frankly, delusional," said Senate Majority Leader Mitch McConnell (R-KY). "It is so unserious that it ought to be beneath one of our two major political parties to line up behind it" (Adragna 2019). McConnell put the Green New Deal resolution to a vote on the Senate floor on March 26, 2019, without allowing any testimony or debate. It was defeated 57–0, with forty-two Democrats and one Independent voting "present" in protest against what they described as a disingenuous political stunt by the majority leader.

Although polls showed broad public support for government action to mitigate the effects of climate change, opponents of the Green New Deal proved more effective than proponents in disseminating their views of the legislation. A survey of likely 2020 voters commissioned by the Green Advocacy Project found that 71 percent of Republicans had heard "a lot" about the Green New Deal, compared to 37 percent of Democrats. Most of the information came from negative reports on the conservative Fox News network, which provided more coverage of the Green New Deal than the mainstream news networks CNN and MSNBC combined (Roberts 2019b). Some observers suggested that Ocasio-Cortez had to prescribe a complete overhaul of the U.S. economic system to overcome such entrenched opposition. "There is simply no way to mount a realistic response to climate change without changing political reality," Eric Levitz wrote in *New York Magazine*. "And for now, the Green New Deal is the most realistic plan we've got for doing the latter" (Levitz 2019).

MODERN MONETARY THEORY

In responding to questions about how she planned to finance her ambitious set of progressive policies, Ocasio-Cortez embraced an unconventional economic concept called modern monetary theory (MMT). MMT rejects the basic notion that the federal government must operate with a balanced budget, which requires new expenditures to be covered by tax increases or spending cuts. Instead, MMT proponents argue that deficit spending is an important tool that enables the federal government to make large-scale public investments that pay off over time. "A deficit isn't a bad thing," said David Roberts of Vox, "it's just a foot on the accelerator" (Roberts 2019a). Contrary to the popular belief that budget deficits harm the economy by causing inflation in the price of goods and services, MMT supporters claim that balanced budget requirements—by limiting government spending—create an underperforming economy characterized by excess capacity, unemployment, and rising inequality.

Advocates of MMT assert that the U.S. government is free to operate without budget constraints because it controls its own currency, meaning that it can always print more money to pay its debts. As Vox writer Dylan Matthews explained, the federal government "can't go bankrupt because that would mean it ran out of dollars to pay creditors; but it can't run out of dollars, because it is the only agency allowed to create dollars. It would be like a bowling alley running out of points to give players" (Matthews 2019). Most traditional economic theories reject the idea of issuing money to finance projects or pay debts, arguing that it devalues the currency and leads to inflation. Under MMT, however, "the U.S. government can spend all the money it wants," according to Roberts. "What ultimately sets the limits on America's ability to invest are its *resources*. It has so much labor potential, so much natural resources, so much manufacturing capacity, etc. By paying for stuff, injecting money into the economy, the government puts those resources to work" (Roberts 2019a). Unlike the traditional economic model, which fights inflation by increasing interest rates, MMT pulls back on government spending or raises taxes to put the brakes on the economy.

Ocasio-Cortez and other MMT supporters view deficit financing as an economic pathway to fund a slate of progressive social reforms, such as universal health care, tuition-free college, and the Green New Deal. They point out that Republican presidents have run up massive budget deficits in the past to finance their priorities, such as tax cuts and defense spending, and say MMT provides Democrats with intellectual justification to do the same. "Democrats have effectively been offering to cooperate and pay for all their budget proposals," Matthews wrote, "even as Republicans repeatedly defect and show no interest in paying for anything. The rational move in such a game is to start defecting yourself. . . . MMT just strengthens Democrats' bargaining position in this regard, as it lets them send a credible signal that they don't even think it's a good idea to pay for everything" (Matthews 2019).

FURTHER READING

Adragna, Anthony. 2019. "GOP Lawmaker: Green New Deal 'Tantamount to Genocide.'" Politico, March 14, 2019. https://www.politico.com/story/2019/03/14/green-new-deal-genocide-1270839.

Beinert, Peter. 2019. "AOC's Generation Doesn't Presume America's Innocence." Atlantic, June 21, 2019. https://www.theatlantic.com/ideas/archive/2019/06/aoc-isnt-interested-american-exceptionalism/592213/.

Belvedere, Matthew J. 2019. "Far-Left Policies from Alexandria Ocasio-Cortez and Some Democratic Presidential Candidates Are 'Dangerous,' Warns Ex-House GOP Leader Eric Cantor." CNBC, March 15, 2019. https://www.cnbc.com/2019/03/15/eric-cantor-far-left-ideas-from-ocasio-cortez-and-2020-dems-dangerous.html.

Cadigan, Hilary. 2018. "Alexandria Ocasio-Cortez Learned Her Most Important Lessons from Restaurants." Bon Appetit, November 7,

2018. https://www.yahoo.com/lifestyle/alexandria-ocasio-cortez-learned-her-141500873.html.

Cheney-Rice, Zak. 2019. "AOC Put a Spotlight on Migrant Detention Conditions. Conservative Media Focused on Her Manners." *New York*, July 2, 2019. http://nymag.com/intelligencer/2019/07/aoc-detention-camp-etiquette.html.

Clark, Dartunorro. 2018. "Alexandria Ocasio-Cortez Credits Talking Issues, Not Trump, for Upset Win in Democratic Primary." NBC News, June 27, 2018. https://www.nbcnews.com/politics/white-house/alexandria-ocasio-cortez-credits-talking-issues-not-trump-upset-win-n886936.

Da Silva, Chantal. 2019. "Alexandria Ocasio-Cortez: College Admissions Scandal Is Proof U.S. Justice System 'Targets Race' and Pardons 'Crimes of Wealth and Privilege.'" *Newsweek*, April 17, 2019. https://www.newsweek.com/alexandria-ocasio-cortez-college-admissions-scandal-proof-us-justice-system-1398912.

Edwards, Jim, and Theron Mohamed. 2019. "Alexandria Ocasio-Cortez Is a Fan of a Geeky Economic Theory Called MMT: Here's a Plain-English Guide to What It Is and Why It's Interesting." *Business Insider*, March 30, 2019. https://www.businessinsider.com/modern-monetary-theory-mmt-explained-aoc-2019-3.

Friedman, Lisa. 2019. "What Is the Green New Deal? A Climate Proposal, Explained." *The New York Times*, February 21, 2019. https://www.nytimes.com/2019/02/21/climate/green-new-deal-questions-answers.html.

Friends of the Earth. 2019. "Progressive Green New Deal Letter to Congress." FOE.org, January 10, 2019. http://foe.org/wp-content/uploads/2019/01/Progressive-Climate-Leg-Sign-On-Letter-2.pdf.

Garcia, Victor. 2019. "Ivanka Trump Challenges Ocasio-Cortez Platform, Says Americans Don't Want 'Guaranteed Minimum.'" Fox News, February 25, 2019. https://www.foxnews.com/politics/ivanka-trump-challenges-ocasio-cortez-platform-says-americans-dont-want-guaranteed-minimum.

Gressier, Roman. 2019. "Ocasio-Cortez: Stop Treating Schools as 'Mini-Jails.'" *Crime Report*, April 21, 2019. https://thecrimereport

.org/2019/04/21/ocasio-cortez-calls-for-renewal-of-justice-values-to-bring-america-home/.

Haltiwanger, John. 2019. "This Is the Platform that Launched Alexandria Ocasio-Cortez, a 29-Year-Old Democratic Socialist, to Become the Youngest Woman Ever Elected to Congress." *Business Insider*, January 4, 2019. https://www.businessinsider.com/alexandria-ocasio-cortez-platform-on-the-issues-2018-6.

Holmes, Jack. 2018. "Fox News Reminds Us Alexandria Ocasio-Cortez's Platform Is . . . Pretty Reasonable." *Esquire*, June 28, 2018. https://www.esquire.com/news-politics/a21985697/sean-hannity-democratic-platform-ocasio-cortez/.

Kurtzleben, Danielle. 2019. "Rep. Alexandria Ocasio-Cortez Releases Green New Deal Outline." NPR, February 7, 2019. https://www.npr.org/2019/02/07/691997301/rep-alexandria-ocasio-cortez-releases-green-new-deal-outline.

Lambiet, Jose. 2019. "Exclusive: 'God Played Quite a Joke on Me with This Politics Stuff.'" *Daily Mail*, March 4, 2019. https://www.dailymail.co.uk/news/article-6748793/Alexandria-Ocasio-Cortezs-mother-tells-hopes-daughter-marries-longtime-boyfriend.html.

Levitz, Eric. 2019. "AOC's Green New Deal Resolution Is Utopian—and Pragmatic." *New York*, February 7, 2019. http://nymag.com/intelligencer/2019/02/ocasio-cortez-aoc-green-new-deal-resolution-explained-utopian-and-pragmatic.html.

Matthews, Dylan. 2019. "Modern Monetary Theory, Explained." Vox, April 16, 2019. https://www.vox.com/future-perfect/2019/4/16/18251646/modern-monetary-theory-new-moment-explained.

McDonald, Andy. 2019. "Alexandria Ocasio-Cortez Calls on Women to 'Shake the Table' in Women's March Speech." *Huffington Post*, January 19, 2019. https://www.huffpost.com/entry/alexandria-ocasio-cortez-womens-march-speech_n_5c437b84e4b0a8dbe171ed19.

Ocasio-Cortez, Alexandria. 2018. "Alexandria Ocasio-Cortez's Platform." Ocasio 2018, https://ocasio2018.com/issues.

116th Congress. 2019. "H. Res. 109—Recognizing the Duty of the Federal Government to Create a Green New Deal." Congress.gov,

February 7, 2019. https://www.congress.gov/bill/116th-congress/house-resolution/109/text.

Paiella, Gabriella. 2018. "The 28-Year-Old at the Center of One of This Year's Most Exciting Primaries." *New York*, June 25, 2018. https://www.thecut.com/2018/06/alexandria-ocasio-cortez-interview.html.

Roberts, David. 2019a. "The Green New Deal, Explained." Vox, March 30, 2019. https://www.vox.com/energy-and-environment/2018/12/21/18144138/green-new-deal-alexandria-ocasio-cortez.

Roberts, David. 2019b. "Fox News Has United the Right against the Green New Deal. The Left Remains Divided." Vox, April 22, 2019. https://www.vox.com/energy-and-environment/2019/4/22/18510518/green-new-deal-fox-news-poll.

Schwartz, Ian. 2019. "Sen. Cotton: Media Complicit in 'Disappearing' Ocasio-Cortez's Green New Deal Gaffe." RealClear Politics, February 12, 2019. https://www.realclearpolitics.com/video/2019/02/12/sen_tom_cotton_media_complicit_in_disappearing_ocasio-cortezs_green_new_deal_gaffe.html.

Serwer, Adam. 2019. "A Crime by Any Name." *Atlantic*, July 3, 2019. https://www.theatlantic.com/ideas/archive/2019/07/border-facilities/593239/.

Warikoo, Niraj. 2019. "Rep. Rashida Tlaib: Migrants 'Treated Like Cattle' in Detention Centers." *Detroit Free Press*, July 8, 2019. https://www.freep.com/story/news/local/michigan/2019/07/08/rashida-tlaib-migrant-detention-border-patrol-camps-texas/1635978001/.

Conclusion

FUTURE OF THE
DEMOCRATIC PARTY

There's always this talk about division within the Democratic Party, ideological differences. But I actually think they're generational differences. Because the America we grew up in is nothing like the America our parents or our grandparents grew up in. (Alter, 2019)

Even among Democrats, Alexandria Ocasio-Cortez became a polarizing figure. Although the freshman congresswoman generated remarkable levels of attention and excitement, she also aroused considerable criticism and controversy. Many observers wondered how her sudden emergence on the national stage would impact her party's future ideological direction and electoral prospects. As a leader of the party's progressive wing, Ocasio-Cortez contributed to a growing tension between liberal Democrats who wanted to put forth a bold vision for change that would energize voters, and moderate Democrats who favored a more gradual approach that would create legislation with a greater likelihood of passing and becoming law. "Ocasio-Cortez threatens the status quo, bringing a youthful impatience to a set of policies popularized by Bernie Sanders's 2016 campaign," Charlotte Alter wrote in a

Time magazine cover story. "She seems more concerned with movements than elections; she doesn't talk about flipping seats and votes, but rather of winning hearts and minds. Hers is the politics of the possible, not the practical" (Alter 2019).

As the youngest woman ever elected to Congress, Ocasio-Cortez also symbolized a generational divide within the party that raised tricky questions about its overall approach. Surveys showed that millennials—who were poised to overtake baby boomers as the largest generation of Americans in 2019—generally felt disenchanted with the nation's political and economic systems, which they tended to view as rigged in favor of wealthy individuals and corporations. In fact, an Axios poll of young people between the ages of 18 and 24 found that a larger proportion expressed positive feelings about socialism (61 percent) than about capitalism (58 percent) (Salmon 2019). Such antiestablishment sentiments contributed to the election of Ocasio-Cortez and Rashida Tlaib (D-MI) as the first two members of the Democratic Socialists of America (DSA) in Congress. Many Democrats disavowed socialism, however, and party leaders struggled to reconcile the different factions and priorities.

SHAKING UP THE STATUS QUO

Even before she took office, Ocasio-Cortez tangled with the most powerful Democrat in the House, Speaker Nancy Pelosi (D-CA), by participating in a climate change protest outside her office. Immediately after the freshman congresswoman was sworn in, she defied party leadership once again by voting against a procedural rule called PAYGO that requires Congress to balance any expenditures with tax increases or spending cuts. "That might sound wildly arcane, but it's actually a fight that reveals the growing power struggle between the Democratic Party's establishment and its insurgent left wing over the very foundation of the party's economic agenda," Jeff Spross noted in *The Week* (Spross 2019). Pelosi went on to make several comments dismissing the influence of Ocasio-Cortez and other high-profile new legislators. Her remarks further fed media speculation about a feud within the party.

Pelosi and other long-serving Democrats argued that Ocasio-Cortez and her fellow progressives lacked the clout—not to mention the votes—to dictate the party's priorities during their first term in Congress. Critics insisted that the newcomers needed to move slowly, pay their dues, and build public support and political coalitions around their policy goals. After all, they pointed out, enacting major progressive reforms would be impossible unless Democrats held the House, gained control of the Senate, and defeated Trump in the 2020 elections. Ocasio-Cortez recognized the need to appeal to swing voters in districts where Democratic lawmakers had to fight to hold their seats against strong Republican challengers. "I think leadership, their primary goal right now is making sure that everyone who won a swing seat comes back," she acknowledged. "So I think that that's where a lot of their time—rightfully, I think, justifiably—is invested, in those relationships" (Remnick 2019).

At the same time, though, Ocasio-Cortez asserted that the passive, incremental approach favored by party leaders had not worked for Democrats in the past—and had, in fact, contributed to Trump's victory in the 2016 presidential race. "I think we became the party of hemming and hawing and trying to be all things to everybody. And it's not to say that we need to exclude people, but it's to say that we don't have to be afraid of having a clear message," she stated. "For me, overall, the plan was to try to expand our national debate and reframe our understanding of issues, because I felt as though that was something that wasn't being done enough, especially on the Democratic side, for Democrats. We don't know how to talk about our own issues in ways that I think are convincing, so we fall into Republican frames all the time. And we're too often on the defensive, we're too often afraid of our own values and sticking up for them. And I feel like we run away from our convictions too much" (Remnick 2019).

ATTRACTING A NEW GENERATION OF VOTERS

Disillusionment over the election of Trump energized the Democratic base and contributed to the "blue wave" that brought Ocasio-Cortez, along with record numbers of women and people of color, to Congress in 2018. Ocasio-Cortez interpreted the midterm election results as a repudiation of Trump's agenda and a mandate for House Democrats to pursue progressive reforms. Proponents of this view pointed out that Democrats had regained control of the House through the overwhelming support of younger voters. Polls showed that two-thirds of voters under age 30 supported Democratic candidates, and that voters under age 45 favored Democrats over Republicans by a 61–36 margin (Rubin 2019). Surveys also found strong support among young Americans for the ideas promoted by Ocasio-Cortez and other progressives, such as Medicare for All, tuition-free public college, and the Green New Deal. "Every year, young people are ticking a couple points more left," said Harvard University political scientist John Della Volpe. "On literally every single question they're moving left" (Alter 2019).

As a millennial, Ocasio-Cortez shared many life experiences with this next generation of Democratic voters, as well as the fundamental sense that U.S. political and economic systems were no longer working for ordinary Americans. "Many millennials don't clearly remember the Reagan-era economic boom," David Byler wrote in *The Washington Post*. "Instead, we have memories of September 11, Hurricane Katrina, the Iraq War, and a recession that caused many to delay marriage, home-buying, and many other rites of passage. It shouldn't be surprising that a generation with those political memories doesn't want to go back to the political past and 'Make America Great Again'" (Byler 2019).

Millennials demonstrated a strong tendency to question institutions and ideas, including the widely accepted premise of American exceptionalism. Unlike previous generations, many young people did not buy into the claim that the United States and its capitalist system, still led primarily by rich white men in the twenty-first century, constituted the only or best option. "A resurgent left fueled by an influx of millennial voters has launched a new challenge to exceptionalist discourse," Peter Beinert wrote in the *Atlantic*. "Partly, it's because a higher percentage of millennials are people of color, who generally look more skeptically on America's claims of moral innocence. Partly, it's because the financial crisis has cast doubt on whether America's economic model is preferable to those practiced in other nations" (Beinert 2019).

Some conservative critics viewed the newcomers calling for progressive changes as ungrateful upstarts who did not appreciate the opportunities they had been afforded by the American political system. A *Wall Street Journal* editorial declared that Ocasio-Cortez "has little regard for the system that made it possible for her to be elected to Congress" and asserted that the congresswoman is leading "a generation of young people [who] take pride in their ignorance—of the laws of nature, of history, of the Constitution, of the eternal battle for freedom—and still succeed" (Turner 2019). Ocasio-Cortez responded by pointing out significant flaws in the U.S. government's record of ensuring freedom and equality for all citizens. "I guess WSJ Editorial Page takes pride in their ignorance of our nation's history of slavery, Jim Crow, & mass incarceration; willful doubt on the decades of science on climate change; targeting of indigenous peoples; and the classist, punitive agenda targeting working families," she tweeted (Mahdawi 2019).

Ocasio-Cortez and many other millennials embraced democratic socialism as a means of overhauling the system to ensure fairness for working people and eliminate economic inequality. "When it comes to democratic socialism, the key word is that small d—democratic," she explained. "It's really about making sure that workers have democratic power in our economy" (Remnick 2019). In Ocasio-Cortez's view, the ideas that conservative critics derided as "socialist" echoed some of the bold reforms enacted by Democratic leaders of the past, such as President Franklin D. Roosevelt's New Deal programs or President Lyndon B. Johnson's Great Society programs. "What we call bold agendas, or Republicans call socialist, are things that they've always called socialist," she noted. "And [we should] wear it, understand that that's what they're going to say, but don't run away from the actual policies that can transform people's lives" (Remnick 2019).

Many Democrats argued, however, that the concept of true socialism was freighted with political baggage and only held appeal for a small subsection of the electorate. "I philosophically disagree with it—not for political reasons but for substantive reasons," said Representative Ro Khanna (D-CA), a leader of the House Progressive Caucus. "If you believe literally, as it's defined, then you would say that government could take over Apple. Let me tell you, that's a horrible idea. I'm very glad that Tim Cook is running Apple" (Relman 2019).

These tensions within the Democratic party are still in evidence. Justice Democrats, the organization that helped Ocasio-Cortez challenge ten-term incumbent Joseph Crowley in 2018, has announced plans to recruit a diverse slate of progressive candidates to mount insurgent primary challenges against moderate Democrats in 2020. Some of the representatives targeted include Henry Cuellar (D-TX), Seth Moulton (D-MA), and Kathleen Rice (D-NY).

This plan has generated anger and resentment among party leaders, who argue that all Democrats should unite behind the goals of expanding their House majority and capturing the Senate and White House. "Do I think this is the best use of our resources, the best use of our star power, the best use of our brain power, going into what very well may be the most important election of our lifetimes?" said political strategist Rodell Mollineau. "I would say that no, this is not it" (Relman 2019). For her part, Ocasio-Cortez has distanced herself from the movement to unseat moderate incumbents in 2020. Nonetheless, she remains the most prominent example of Justice Democrats' strategy for pushing the party down a more progressive path.

As one of the most visible Democrats on the national stage, Ocasio-Cortez seems certain to wield significant influence over her party's future direction. "It's not just that Ocasio-Cortez is pushing for more progressive policies. She's recast the division between left and center as a tug-of-war between the party's past and its future," Alter wrote. "She's not thinking about how to keep the Democratic majority for another two years; she's thinking about how to define the agenda for the next two decades" (Alter 2019).

Some admirers hope the charismatic congresswoman's rise to power heralds the arrival of a new progressive era in American politics. Ocasio-Cortez, however, has expressed more modest goals. "I do hope that the future of the party is in big organizing," she stated. "I hope that the future of the party is in rejecting lobbyist funds. I do hope that the future of the party is in intersectional and unapologetic arguments for economic, social, and racial justice for working-class Americans. Those three things I hope are the future of the Democratic Party. I'm going to work really hard to make that happen" (Feller 2018).

FURTHER READING

Alter, Charlotte. 2019. "'Change Is Closer Than We Think.' Inside Alexandria Ocasio-Cortez's Unlikely Rise." *Time*, March 21, 2019. https://time.com/longform/alexandria-ocasio-cortez-profile/.

Beinert, Peter. 2019. "AOC's Generation Doesn't Presume America's Innocence." *Atlantic*, June 21, 2019. https://www.theatlantic .com/ideas/archive/2019/06/aoc-isnt-interested-american-excep tionalism/592213/.

Byler, David. 2019. "Millennials Could Push American Politics to the Left, or Totally Upend Them." *The Washington Post*, May 22, 2019. https://www.washingtonpost.com/opinions/2019/05/22/ millennials-could-push-american-politics-left-or-totally-upend-them/?utm_term=.1573f957baf7.

Feller, Madison. 2018. "Alexandria Ocasio-Cortez Knows She Can't Save America All by Herself." *Elle*, July 16, 2018. https://www.elle.com/culture/career-politics/a22118408/ alexandria-ocasio-cortez-interview/.

Freedlander, David. 2019. "There Is Going to Be a War within the Party. We Are Going to Lean into It." Politico, February 4, 2019. https://www.politico.com/magazine/story/2019/02/04/the-insurgents-behind-alexandria-ocasio-cortez-224542.

Mahdawi, Arwa. 2019. "Ocasio-Cortez Outrages Republicans by Refusing to Respect Their Ignorance." *Guardian*, March 2, 2019. https://www.theguardian.com/world/2019/mar/02/alexand ria-ocasio-cortez-republicans-ignorance.

Relman, Eliza. 2019. "The Truth about Alexandria Ocasio-Cortez." *Insider*, January 6, 2019. https://www.thisisinsider.com/alexand ria-ocasio-cortez-biography-2019-1.

Remnick, David. 2019. "Alexandria Ocasio-Cortez on the 2020 Presidential Race and Trump's Crisis at the Border." *New Yorker*, July 10, 2019. https://www.newyorker.com/news/the-new-yorker-interview/alexandria-ocasio-cortez-on-the-2020-presidential-race-and-trumps-crisis-at-the-border.

Rubin, Jennifer. 2019. "The Anti-Trump Generation Engages." *The Washington Post*, April 24, 2019. https://www.washing tonpost.com/opinions/2019/04/24/anti-trump-generation-engages/?utm_term=.65c085ff8458.

Salmon, Felix. 2019. "Gen Z Prefers Socialism to Capitalism." Axios, January 27, 2019. https://www.axios.com/socialism-capital ism-poll-generation-z-preference-1ffb8800-0ce5-4368-8a6f-de3b82662347.html.

Spross, Jeff. 2019. "What Is PAYGO and Why Are Democrats Fighting over It?" *The Week*, January 4, 2019. https://theweek.com/articles/815501/what-paygo-why-are-democrats-fighting-over.

Turner, Grace-Marie. 2019. "Alexandria Ocasio-Cortez Is an All-American Socialist." *The Wall Street Journal*, February 26, 2019. https://www.wsj.com/articles/ocasio-cortez-is-an-all-american-socialist-11551225829.

INDEX

About the Author

LAURIE COLLIER HILLSTROM is a writer and editor based in Brighton, Michigan. She is the author of more than forty books in the areas of American history, biography, politics, and current events, including *The #MeToo Movement, The Vaping Controversy, Defining Moments: The Stonewall Riots, School Shootings and the Never Again Movement,* and *Black Lives Matter: From a Moment to a Movement.*